The
FLY
FISHERMAN'S
GUIDE *to the*
MEANING *of* LIFE

Titles in the
GUIDES *to the* MEANING *of* LIFE
series

— The —
FLY FISHERMAN'S
GUIDE *to the*
MEANING *of* LIFE

WHAT A LIFETIME ON THE WATER
HAS TAUGHT ME ABOUT LOVE, WORK,
FOOD, SEX, AND GETTING UP EARLY

PETER KAMINSKY
AUTHOR OF *THE MOON PULLED UP AN ACRE OF BASS*

RODALE

© 2002 by Peter Kaminsky

All rights reserved. No part of this publication may be reproduced or transmitted in any form or by any means, electronic or mechanical, including photocopying, recording, or any other information storage and retrieval system, without the written permission of the publisher.

Guides to the Meaning of Life is a trademark of Rodale Inc.

Printed in the United States of America

Rodale Inc. makes every effort to use acid-free ∞, recycled paper ♺.

Dark Hendrickson dry fly pictured on cover tied by Gavin Robinson; pattern first tied in 1916 by Roy Steenrod

Cover Series Designer: Lee Fukui
Cover Designer: Joanna Williams
Cover Photographer: Mitch Mandel/Rodale Images

Library of Congress Cataloging-in-Publication Data

Kaminsky, Peter.
    The fly fisherman's guide to the meaning of life : what a lifetime on the water has taught me about love, work, food, sex, and getting up early / by Peter Kaminsky.
        p.   cm.
   ISBN 1–57954–584–X hardcover
   1. Quality of life.   2. Fly fishing—Miscellanea.   I. Title.
BF637.C5 K35 2002
170'.44—dc21
                                            2002002552

Distributed to the book trade by St. Martin's Press

2   4   6   8   10   9   7   5   3   1   hardcover

Visit us on the Web at www.rodalestore.com,
or call us toll-free at (800) 848-4735.

RODALE

WE **INSPIRE** AND **ENABLE** PEOPLE TO IMPROVE
THEIR LIVES AND THE WORLD AROUND THEM

For Lucy and Lily

Acknowledgments

First, thanks to the fish: I love them all. Also, to every angler who ever shared time on the water with me. To my friend, representative, and fellow scotch fancier, Mark Reiter. His colleagues, Anne Torrago and Charity Bustamente. Laurent Gras for a recipe that works all the time. Horsewoman Stephanie Tade, who basically said, "Let it rock!"

And, ever and always, Melinda.

Contents

— The —
FLY
FISHERMAN'S
GUIDE *to the*
MEANING *of* LIFE

Pleasure and Instinct

**WHAT THE VIEW FROM BEHIND
A FLY ROD CAN TEACH YOU ABOUT
TIME, HUMANITY, AND EXISTENCE**

I have always thought it very wise on the part of Thomas Jefferson, John Hancock, and the rest of the founding fathers that they included the phrase "the pursuit of happiness" in the Declaration of Independence. They weren't so foolhardy as to promise the fulfillment of happiness, only its pursuit. Nobody can guarantee happiness, anymore than anyone can guarantee the outcome of a baseball game, an election, a dinner date, or a war. All of these things must be played out. So it is with fly fishing. As the English poet Matthew Arnold observed in "Sohrab and Rustum," a tale of combat and struggle that I had to memorize in the tenth grade, "Only the event itself will teach us in its hour."

The fly rod is the tool I use in my pursuit of happiness, and a very particular kind of happiness it is. When I have a fly rod in my hand and water all around me, time stops. Let me try that again: Time doesn't so much stop as it passes in a different way. I enter a different reality, one in which I am fully alive, fully focused, where each second is a ripe fruit bursting with juice. This is true of all things that bring us pleasure, whether it is making love or making bread, hitting a homerun or cheering for one, playing golf or reading a novel, or driving with the top down, Muddy Waters blasting on the radio. Some of these moments you will remember as fully as hours, days, even whole years in "real life."

Then, when you are through with your plea-sure—after the last cast, the last putt, the last note of the symphony—you have the feeling of waking up, a sense that the whole experience passed in an instant. Luckily, the next time you go fishing you return to the state of mind you were in when you last picked up a rod. Time passes on two tracks: one for everyday life and one for when you transcend life's constant cares and pressures and find your pleasure.

Each sense of time ignores the other. They are antithetical—one bogged down in the huge hassle involved in making a living, getting the kids to school on time, having your teeth cleaned, taking a dressing down from your boss. And in that other time—pleasure time—it is just you and the world, moving in synch, not always succeeding but always having the possibility of success. It is once-upon-a-time time, not anchored to a particular date but feeling like it is part of that same time when Zeus was hurling thunderbolts on his worshippers, when elves dug burrows for their pots of gold, when King Arthur and his knights sat around the round table feasting on bitter ale and roast haunch of whatever the forest yielded up to the bowman that day.

Not that I compare my time on the water with the exploits of legend and myth, but when I am fly fishing I have the same feeling about time as I do

when I hear those ancient stories. They all coexist
in an eternal and much more interesting present
than the workaday one in which you and I pass
most of life.

I have learned all of this through fly fishing:
not necessarily because it is the contemplative, soul-
enriching experience that many fisherfolk have ar-
gued that it is (largely, I think, to excuse their
obsessive pursuit of what nonanglers think of as
"goofing off"). For the most part, that highfalutin
school of writing is flowery fluff, self-justification
from an era when pleasure was regarded as suspect
so men—it was usually men who got to indulge in
pleasures in the old days—went through all kinds of
mental gymnastics to show how their pastimes
brought them closer to God. I will admit, though,
that sometimes when I am fishing I feel moments of
transcendence. I remember a day floating over the
emerald waters of a coral flat in the Florida Keys and
being lost in myself and thinking, "This is probably
the way William Blake felt when he was inspired to
paint his images of Gods and demons." But more

often fishing just brings me pleasure as comfortable and easy as an old flannel shirt. It feels right and always has since the first day I picked up a fly rod.

I am happy when I am fishing, when I get off a good cast, when I have the sense that the fly is sailing to a patch of water that looks—well, the only word I can use to describe it is *pregnant*. When that happens my happiness turns to pleasure, involving my whole being in something I love and which I could not, at that moment, imagine forsaking for anything else.

It often happens that when I am interviewed about fishing, someone says, "It looks so peaceful and Zen. Is that what you get out of fishing?" I think that the question, which is completely well-meaning, often comes from having seen Robert Redford's movie adaptation of *A River Runs through It*, with Brad Pitt waving his rod in the air, his line shooting out like a laser, the sun lighting up the golden spray off the line, the lush music underneath—that is Hollywood fly fishing.

Mine is a more simple faith. I do it because it

makes me feel whole. I do it, when you get right down to brass tacks, because it is what I do, what I am about. If I don't fish, the rest of life is that much harder to handle. It is recreation, but it is also a re-*creation*. So my answer to the well-meaning interviewer often is, "I can't really say why I like fly fishing. Ask me instead about other things I like and I will answer: 'They make me feel as good as I do when I have a fly rod in my hand.' My pleasure starts with fly fishing, and I measure everything else by it. It is my first principle."

In that way, fly fishing is for me what golf or sailing or cooking or wine collecting or growing roses or taking a walk with your child is for others. But it is more than that. I bet you knew at some point I would get around to fessing up to the fact that I recognize that people get an equal charge out of other pastimes but that I think mine is a little more special. Like the other things we pursuers of happiness spend our time pursuing, fly fishing is pleasant; it is a skill one can perfect all through life, a basis for camaraderie and friendship, but that doesn't tell the whole tale.

We humans are born with two drives. One is to feed ourselves. The other is to make the next generation, i.e., sex. Fly fishing falls into the first category, the finding food category. Humans evolved as hunters. Anthropologists conjecture that skills of communication, hand-eye coordination, and tool making evolved as we became more efficient hunters. "Hunt" in the sense of seeking out as one does for mushrooms or berries as well as "hunt" in the sense of pursuing a quarry, capturing it, and consuming it. Brutal, but a fundamental aspect of human nature.

The fly fisherman or -woman, then, combines the artistry and refinement of a wonderful game with the primal hunting instinct that quickens every pulse, makes every heart beat faster, focuses every spirit on the moment of action. Even if you don't hunt and never plan to, you have this instinct in you, which—when I see a bonefish cruising a coral flat or a trout making the subtlest of rings as it feeds on mayflies in a placid stream or a pack of tarpon approaching like wolves on the prowl—I am thrilled and intent in a way that absorbs my whole being.

Find food, make babies—isn't that the meaning of life? There may be more to it, according to what god or gods you bow down to, but without those drives there is no life. So fly fishing, that refined and tweedy sport first perfected by port-swilling rich English gents, is one of the very few things we can do that connects us directly to the emotions of our Cro-Magnon ancestors and their Neanderthal forbearers and back and back, before history, to all of the creatures on our family tree until we reach that dusty gorge in Kenya where a little woman that archeologists named Lucy first stood on her hind legs, looked across the savannah, and took the steps that have brought us to the world we have made.

René Descartes, that wise French philosopher, once said, "I think, therefore I am." Peter Kaminsky, fly fisherman from Brooklyn, New York, would humbly rephrase that: "I think about fishing, therefore I am human."

The Measure of Success

**YOU FAIL MORE
THAN YOU SUCCEED**

Some years ago I went fishing in northern Florida, on the St. Johns River to be exact. It was a wild watery wilderness with swift-moving flowages connecting a chain of lakes rich in game fish. Eagles and osprey snagged small striped bass, bluegill, largemouth, and even flounder in this mixed fishery. Most wondrous of all, huge huffing manatees as big as horses—very chubby horses—bobbed up everywhere. My fishing partner was John Madison Culler, at that time the editor of *Outdoor Life* magazine, in which position he bought my first fishing story. John didn't stay in New York too long; Yankee ways and Yankee winters did not agree with his country boy soul.

John invited me on a tour of the South, fishing our way down from South Carolina through Georgia to Florida. It was late March. The bass and bluegill were getting ready to spawn and, in that agitated condition, were gloriously catchable. John, who fished live bait on a casting reel, caught a twelve-pound largemouth bass, the largest one I have ever seen taken.

But that is not what stands out most clearly. My most vivid memory on that trip is of the fellows with Tennessee license plates who had come down to fish shellcrackers, copperbreasts, and numerous other local varieties of bluegills known by numerous other local names—all delicious when coated with breadcrumbs and deep-fried in hot oil. (Of course, a phone book would probably taste great too . . . if you breaded and deep-fried it.)

"How's the fishing, boys?" I inquired.

"We started early and by nine o'clock, we were

back in the trailer with three hundred fish in the cooler."

When they left three days later, they estimated that they had iced down about three thousand fish. There would be some fish fry back in Knoxville.

I liked those guys. I had no problem with them taking so many bluegill; the river could well support it. But their measure of angling success and the fly fisherman's are quite different, and therein lies a life lesson, certainly an angling lesson: It is not how many you catch, but how you catch them and what you catch that counts. In fly fishing, the quality of the experience far outweighs the quantity of fish you catch. In fact, dismiss the word *count* from your vocabulary.

This brings us back to the pursuit of happiness. No sane person is happy all the time. Likewise, not even the best angler catches fish all the time. Look at it this way: In major league baseball, a so-so hitter will carry an average of .250. That means he will get a hit twenty-five out of a hundred times at bat. A good hitter may bat .300. The difference, then, between nothing special and an All-Star is only five hits for every hundred appearances. Even more telling, our All-Star fails seven out of ten times, and the world considers this good!

Fly fishing holds true to this same pattern. You fail more than you succeed. One cast out of ten, or twenty, or a hundred may produce a strike at the other end of the line. (Mark Twain said of fishing, "It is a jerk at one end of the line waiting for a jerk at the other end.") And then, when a fish does take the fly, you must set the hook, fight it well, and not let it break your leader with its leaps and runs and dives under a rock or branch.

All in all, the odds are against you big time. Still, the pursuit excites. If your goal is in sight, you can spend a whole afternoon striving and not hooking up, yet you may go home that day feeling you have had pleasure in casting your fly.

There was an afternoon in Montana on a spring creek that I fished with Doug McClelland. The waters of this creek in the valley of Yellowstone run clear and at a constant temperature year-round. Its limestone geology makes for a particularly rich food chain, starting with microorganisms and algae and working on up to a profusion of mayflies and fat happy trout that feed on them.

The particular stretch we fished that day was as near to pristine as you can get: The visitor's log revealed that only five anglers had cast a fly there from the first of the year until the ninth of August. No way these fish had grown used to man's feathery offerings.

You could see the trout, sleek and healthy, rising rhythmically, dimpling the water as they sipped the delicate and beautiful Pale Morning Duns, mayflies with bodies a faded yellow like afternoon light in the winter and their upright wings a wispy purple of the kind that paints the sky just before dusk turns to dark.

I waded in and cast my fly on a long delicate leader. The fly landed as soft as a falling leaf and floated into the feeding lane of the trout. Time slowed as the fly came within a trout's view; the trout rose in the water, looked at the fly, and de-scended.

No problem. I changed flies and tried again, with the same result. Still, I was heartened that my presentation was delicate enough that I could keep the interest of the trout and not spook him. I spent an hour or two or three—there's that thing about time again—casting to that fish. I never did hook him, but still he and I had a fine encounter. It was like fencing when nobody succeeds in marking the opponent. Does that make it a bad match? Quite the contrary; two good fencers suc-ceeded in countering every thrust, parry, and lunge of the opponent.

The fact that it all happened in plain view made the experience memorable, more memorable than a thousand other times that I have actually succeeded in catching a fish. I suppose, however, that if I had not been able to observe the beautiful trout, finning, rising, taking natural insects, and from time to time examining mine, I would not

have looked at this fishless fishing session as memorable.

Nor, to be honest, would a steady diet of such
futility satisfy me much. I need to catch the occasional fish because that is the point of the exercise,
but how many, how often, and how big are subjec-
tive questions.

For me, the difference between no fish and
one fish is vastly greater than the difference between one fish and a hundred. That one fish means
that the day can be entered in the memory bank in
the account labeled "Success." As Al Caucci, whom
many consider to be the most influential modern
American trout fisherman, has often observed on
days when we don't catch many fish, "One fabulous
hour of fishing can make a week."

Al had many opportunities to share his
wisdom with me in the course of a windswept week
of rolling seas off Montauk, Long Island. It was the
heart of the season, the peak of the run, when the
striped bass take over the ocean and darken the wa-

ters along the shore in their millions to feed on little
green anchovies that likewise congregate by the bil-
lions in the churning currents between the Gulf
Stream and Montauk Point.

Al had expressed an interest in visiting me
during the time when the fishing was as close as it
could be to a sure thing. But of course, neither in
fishing nor in life is there ever a sure thing. On day
one we tried to motor around the Point, but turbu-
lent swells rose in front of us, one of them knocking
Al off his feet, resulting in a heart-stopping conk on
the head. Cooch, a former high school running
back, shook it off with a brusque "I'm all right."

The next day the wind blew harder. The fish
were there—you could see them as we drove the
beach—but there was no way Al wanted to venture
out in these conditions, and I agreed. Day two,
strike two.

On day three Al was supposed to go back
home to Pennsylvania to attend to business (he runs
a lovely lodge on the west branch of the Delaware
River, one of the premier trout waters in the East).

Business could wait, he told me. He knew there were fish to be had, if only the conditions were right. And when there are that many fish around and you are a fisherman, you know that eventually you will cast your fly to them, so you wait and hope for that one fabulous hour.

Day four: The whole philosophical approach was getting kind of old by this point, but flocks of screeching gulls diving to massed bait through which thousands of bass moved with murderous precision kept us hoping and longing like men on a chain gang watching a pretty girl pass by.

Friday, the seas laid down and we booked our friend Wally Jensen's boat, the most stable and most seaworthy in the Montauk fly rod fleet.

Now we were sure to slay 'em.

But the fish hadn't read the script. The feeding frenzy that we had watched from afar was over. Maybe the winds had finally driven the bait off-shore and the bass had followed. Maybe the particular herd of stripers we had been watching for the last four days had decided to make its way

south, and we were in a lull until the next mass of
fish appeared.

At three o'clock that afternoon, perilously
close to the time when Al would have to forsake
even that one redemptive hour, the light showed
golden in the west. The tide flowed out past the
Montauk lighthouse, and a rip set up where the currents ran into undersea hills and valleys. Very fishy
looking, so we looked. And looked. And looked.

Then, right behind us, Wally noticed a splotch
of red under the water, the characteristic color of
massing rainbait when the bass have surrounded
them. The color spread, like a wine stain on a white
tablecloth. It deepened in hue and then soared up
from the depths and exploded on the surface.

Bass! Thousands of them, all around us. Mad
with bloodlust. Heedless of our boat. They banged
against it with their bodies as they chomped their
way through the ball of bait. I thought of it as a sea-
coast version of the black holes that occur across
the universe, from which no light escapes. Here the
bass were so concentrated that no bait could escape.

To be present at such a riot of life is to feel more alive than you have ever felt. Your breath comes quickly, your heart pounds. The spray and sun, the smell of bait like fresh-cut cucumbers on the wind. Life takes its meaning from moments like this. We creatures of hunting and gathering have that message in our genes; to partake of it is to drink from the wellsprings of life on this living planet.

And Al had his one fabulous hour and truly, his week was made. Mine too.

FLY FISHING'S
TRANSCENDENT MOMENTS

Everything we love has something we especially treasure at the heart of it, some experience that imprints itself on the soul and attaches you to it. Subsequently, the bonds of affection, even obsession, grow ever stronger. Though such moments are rare, they are the payoff. These are mine.

THE YANKEE STADIUM VIEW

Turn back the clock, way back, to my first visit to the high temple of major league baseball on 161st Street in the Bronx. I was nine. In those days, we had a black-and-white TV. I remember walking into the stadium: lots of kids saying "Buy me this, Daddy"; old guys smoking cigars down to impossibly short butts; the organ blaring; and all of that cacophony echoing off the concrete innards of the stadium. As we entered the walkway to our $1.75 grandstand seats, I could see a patch of blue sky. We proceeded. Then green field and white uniforms, finally opening out onto a panorama of green. "My God," I thought, "it's in color!"

Likewise, tramping through the woods in the cool, misty predawn. Startled deer bound from their pine-needle beds; the last call of the owl; then the sound of rushing water, louder and louder until, like the walkway at Yankee Stadium, the path opens out onto a view of the river. The first shafts of sunlight hit the water and, like dust rising, the bugs are hatching off the surface and I know—more certainly than I know anything—that there will be trout here.

SAILING THROUGH THE SKY

Birth is miraculous, rebirth more so. Though a stream is a living system, when there are no bugs in the water you would swear that it is sterile. But sometime during the day—the great fly fisher Doug Swisher has identified it as the time when the temperature is most pleasant to humans—something stirs beneath the surface. You see flashes of white: trout belly. They feed on nymphs floating in the water. The nymphs ready themselves to hatch. For a year, these immature mayflies have crawled around the dark, cold, rocky stream bottom. Today is the day they will sprout wings, fly into the warm air, make love for the first and last time, and then die. How I would like to sprout wings and make love on my last day on earth, I think.

Just then, like a bright silk kerchief emerging out of a magician's hat, a mayfly pops up through the surface of the water. Though it is no bigger than a quarter, your eyes are caught by it and your spirit lifted. With its upright wings, translucent and pastel, it looks like a sailboat seen from a great height.

Then, continuing the magic act, where there was one sail there are now two, then three, then a flotilla riding the currents in the stream. One after another, they make ready to take wing. Unsteady at first, like colts attempting their first ungainly steps, they whirl about tipsily. The air is full of mayflies now. Some hit the water after a moment in the air, bounce a few times, and try a second takeoff. Some make it the first try. The whole scene reminds me of an old spiritual that Bill Monroe sang in the 1930s:

> I'm gonna take a trip
>
> On that old gospel ship;
>
> I'm going far beyond the sky.
>
> I'm gonna shout and sing,
>
> Until the bells do ring,
>
> When I'm sailing through the sky.

By now the trout have taken notice, and they begin to pick off the mayflies before they get a chance to test their wings, which catch the sunlight like jewels. The trout feed in rhythm. You can hear the deep slurp of a big trout and watch the rings of water spread from the spot where it sucked in a mayfly. Hendricksen, March Brown, Green Drake, Blue Winged Olive— names that might hang over the door of a welcoming pub. When the mayfly hatch and the trout are on the feed and you are there—well, then you bless those little living boats.

SHADOWS IN THE FLORIDA KEYS

The day will be hot, but the stars are still out in the clear tropic sky when you leave the dock. If you get there first, nothing will have disturbed the procession of tarpon in packs of ten, twenty, a hundred, moving along in the coral green waters southward to Key West to feast on the full-moon hatch of red palolo worms. It is midtide, and there's a mere breath of wind. Dawn breaks blood red to our right, where Cuba waits over the horizon. To the left, mangroves and white coral, the indeterminate edge of the Keys where the land doesn't so

Fly Fishing's Transcendent Moments

much end as it just stops trying and becomes ocean. Ahead there are glints on the flat water, like light reflected off flashing sabres. Tarpon?

The guide drops his voice: "I see shadows coming toward us at three hundred yards." But you don't see a thing. You are not a guide; you still have city eyes. Then—yes!—silhouettes shaped like torpedoes, the biggest fish you will ever take on a fly. Will they bear down on you and give you a cast? Behind them, more shadows, and on and on as far as you can see—shadows and flaring sunlight. You stand on the casting platform and hope to hell the tarpon don't hear your heart thumping like a kettledrum. And then you let fly for all you are worth.

ABOUT TWO BUCKS WORTH OF PURE PLEASURE

Most of the time, even if the fishing is great right outside your door, the unwritten law of angling is that you drive for somewhere between forty-five minutes and two hours to get to the day's fishing grounds. Must be something about the grass being greener, or El Dorado waiting over the next hill, or the inborn need to drive.

Everyone is asleep in the house, so you don't rattle around the kitchen. You throw your clothes on, don't tie your sneakers, and go out the door within five minutes of the alarm clock going off. It takes a while for the car heater to warm up.

Then you stop at the first Quickie Mart you pass for the biggest cup of coffee they make and a Hershey's bar with almonds. Bitter almonds, sweet chocolate, strong coffee. Sipping, eating, driving with the radio on—and nothing on the agenda but fishing.

WESTERN LIGHT

When the afternoon sun sinks until it is just above the bill of your hat and you look away from it, the sea foam will take on the colors of stained glass. Then, through the incoming swells, the sunlight lights up the forms of fish. To see inside a wave and then to witness life and death—for the fish are always feeding when they are near the surface—is a glimpse into nature that is almost voyeuristic; not dirty, mind you, but to something you feel you weren't intended to see and, when you do see it, it leaves you slack jawed.

The albacore come up this way off the Montauk lighthouse. Their bigger brothers on the Outer Banks of North Carolina do the same thing. In albacore season the wind often comes from the southwest, so you must turn around and face the sun and send a backcast at the swirl of a feeding fish. As you turn, momentarily sunblind, you feel a rewarding *thunk*. The albie takes the fly and is off on a hundred-yard run. You hold on as your reel sings with the angry buzz of a pack of hornets.

FRESH AND HOT

The fish hits the pan in bubbling brown butter, or is roasted with tomatoes, olives, and fresh herbs, or grilled with coarse sea salt on the crust, or steamed over an outdoor fire with damp seaweed mounded on it. Cook it just a few minutes, until it flakes, and serve it up with beer in an iced glass or a crisp Montrachet—go ahead and break out the pricey stuff for the fish you caught all by yourself—or, throwing convention to the wind, try a dark and funky Burgundy. There is no food that tastes fresher, or better, or fills you with the pride of The Provider than something you have caught.

I often hear, "I don't know why, but it always tastes better when you catch it and cook it yourself." I know why. Because it's fresh, fresh, fresh. When people say they don't like the fishy taste of fish, what they mean is they don't like the taste that fish gets after its oils are exposed to air. Neither do I, but even a bluefish or a mackerel is light and clean tasting when it is just hours from the ocean.

The moment of grace, of course, is that first bite, after you've flaked away a forkful, watched the steam rise, and smelled the perfume of flesh born in the river and sea.

THE SLAP

There are days when golfers hit longer drives, when baseball players see the pitch in slow-mo, when every forehand comes off the racquet with the report of a howitzer. When casting and your timing is right, you are neither rushing nor waiting too long. You load up the rod so that you feel it bend all the way down to the grip, then you push it forward feeling it unflex as you pull down hard on the line and double haul for dear life. When you really hit it like that, you know it by the sound of the line racing through the guides: *tic-tic-tic*. The cast unrolls and takes flight. Then, at its limit, the cast pulls the line—*slap*—against the reel. That slap is reserve power.

You have just let fly a textbook cast, a short film of physics in motion. The slap and slight rebound of the line tells you that the cast wanted to go farther, and you have the satisfaction of knowing that you cast so well that, un-mindful of your power, you could have let even more line go. To know that your best was even better than you'd hoped is enough satisfaction to get you through the self-esteem dip that comes with wind knots and sloppy back-casts. Take all the joy you can from the good one. Replay that short film in your head until you can call it up at will, and the next time things don't go as right as you had hoped, try and relive it.

THE RIVER OF GRASS

"There are no other Everglades in the world," Marjory Stoneman Douglas famously wrote. This giant sheet of water drains out of Lake Okechobee and moves about a foot a day as it slides south off the tip of Florida. To come across a place of Jurassic primitiveness in glitzy, overbuilt, over-malled South Florida is always soul restoring. The gators on the banks slip swiftly into the water with a symphonic swoosh; ibis and egret and flamingo take flight, their huge wings lit from above; feeding bream make smooching sounds on the surface, like they're throwing Hollywood air kisses; and the slap of a largemouth bass signals the swallowing of some hapless and delicious creature.

You cast your bug low, letting it bounce under some overhanging sawgrass where the water from the heart of the Glades drains into a canal dug by the Army Corps of Engineers, carrying bait and drawing bass. Let the bug sit there until the rings that it makes upon landing disappear. Then twitch the bug and make it burble while drawing it slowly toward you. Something pushes a bow wave ahead of it

Fly Fishing's Transcendent Moments

as it gathers speed, charging your popper. A big mouth opens, and you strike! "Unh! You sonofabitch," you declaim with impunity because there is no one there to tell you to mind your tongue. And then, the bass is airborne, tailwalking, shaking its head, putting on a performance of fierce gymnastics. The gators stare through lidless eyes, unimpressed.

Ethics and Free Will

**TO CHOOSE NOT TO KILL IS
ONE ELEMENT OF OUR *HUMAN* NATURE**

At first blush, a sport that measures success by ripping a creature from its environment, putting it in fear for its life, and sometimes taking that life would seem to have more to do with survival of the fittest than more soulful notions such as ethics and principles. But there is a lot of right and wrong in fly fishing, and the right carries over into much else that humans have the choice of doing rightly or wrongly.

First, it breeds a respect for life. Contrary to what you might intuit, fishers and hunters have been the leaders in conservation in America, and

America has led the world. Theodore Roosevelt fished and hunted and built the National Park Service. John Audubon hunted birds his whole life. He also created inspiring art that has moved generations of bird lovers. It was hunters who brought back the bison, fishers who brought back the striped bass and the redfish.

Part of this conservation is pure practicality. If you kill everything, you will have no quarry to seek. Just as much, though, there is a deeper connection, almost holy, between predators and prey. The drawings that our ancestors left on Ice Age cave walls were surely of creatures they sought to kill, but just as much, they reflect wonder, respect, and awe at the animals of the ancient tundra.

It was fly fishing that created the idea of catch-and-release. "Limit your kill, don't kill your limit" is the way I have heard it succinctly and powerfully put. This doesn't make the fly fisher morally superior to the deer hunter because, in fairness, you can't very well shoot a deer dead and then let it go. We fly fishers release our fish because we can. Choosing not to take a life, when there is no reason to kill, is moral and right.

To use a resource and not deplete it is seemingly a paradox, but that, for the most part, is what fly fishers do. This is a far cry from the way things were a hundred fifty years ago among so-called sportsmen when gunners massacred an estimated one hundred million buffalo on the Great Plains. Shortly thereafter, they dispatched close to six hundred million passenger pigeons, until one old bird— Martha was her name—languished and died in a Cincinnati zoo.

This wanton destruction of life gave rise, particularly in America, to the idea of fair chase, of taking a shot only when you have a clean one, of never leaving a wounded animal to die of an injury inflicted by a sportsman. It also gave rise to the idea of catch-and-release fishing.

People who do not fish may not understand why you would go through all the trouble of catching something just to let it go. As I indicated earlier, the simple answer is this: Because we can.

So, although I love the flavor of wild trout, I have not killed one in nearly twenty years. A few times I have intended to take a trout or two home for the pan, but at the moment of truth I chose not to.

Although fishing, as I have suggested, fulfills a longing in our animal nature, it is also true that to choose not to kill is one element of our human nature. All animals exploit resources. Only humans are *occasionally* enlightened enough to conserve them.

Before we give ourselves too many pats on the back, however, I should point out that this noble act is also a practical one. "You don't burn your golf balls," is the way my friend and fellow angler Paul Dixon puts it.

In rivers and streams, where the practice of catch-and-release first took hold, anglers fish primarily for trout. In most streams, trout are what is known as a top predator. There is nothing in a stream that feeds on a trout—at least for the most part. True, the occasional otter or raccoon or bear will capture a trout, but that is more the exception than the rule.

The thing about top predators is that, compared to prey, there are relatively few of them. There are more impala than lions, more rabbits than wolves, more minnows than trout. Consequently, it takes very little fishing pressure to degrade a trout fishery. Anglers who were passionate about their sport realized that you could not have your trout and eat him too, and so catch-and-release caught on.

Like many good and practical ideas, when raised to the level of dogma it can become a straightjacket. If catch-and-release is an example of let live, then not lecturing or looking down on the person who keeps the occasional trout for the pan is an equally valid example of live and let live.

Before I venture into these roilsome waters, let me be very clear: I prefer that people not kill trout . . . ever.

Still, the idea of catch-and-release, a noble and moral one, needs to stand alongside the idea of peaceful coexistence, another equally human virtue. That was brought home to me on a trip to Argentina.

It was a cold, windy, very rainy day at the *boca* (mouth) of the Chimehuin, a fabled river in equally fabulous Patagonia. It had not rained for eighty-some days before the skies decided to open up with the Patagonian version of what folks in the Ozarks call a gullywasher—a real soaker.

The rain woke up the trout in Lake Huechu-lafquén and reminded them that it was time to begin their spawning run into the Chimehuin. Trout up to twenty-nine pounds have been taken in the swirling waters of the Chimehuin. The particular spot where we were fishing that day was hallowed ground among the first generation of fly fishers in Argentina, giants of the sport such as the elegant polo and fishing enthusiast Bebe Anchorena, the American big-fish hunter Joe Brooks, the Floridian tarpon and marlin legend Billy Pate, and the Polish nobleman Charles Radziwill.

After World War II, Radziwill, having little en-thusiasm for communism and boundless passion for fly fishing, moved to Argentina and fished often on the Chimehuin, where we came upon him that rainy morning.

He introduced himself. "I'm Charlie Radziwill," he said.

I liked that. There are very few princes who have offered me the opportunity to call them Charlie. He was a lefty caster with an old-fashioned up and down European stroke, as different from the three-quarter sidearm and open stance of the American caster as dressage is from bronco busting. Still, he could pick up the whole line, carry all ninety feet of it in the air, and lay it all out again—quite a feat. In fact, the only other person I have seen do that is Ted Williams.

My friend and guide Bob White sent out a cast as far as Charlie's. At the end of his leader was a smallish Elk Hair Caddis, a dry fly about the size of a horsefly. The Caddis was dwarfed as it rode the rushing current, but it was big enough to catch the attention and awaken the appetite of an eight-pound brown trout.

Bob hooked the fish and Radziwill rushed over. What Charlie didn't know about Bob is that he is one of the greatest American fishing guides and that he had spent two years in Patagonia. As far as Radziwill was concerned, though, this was one lucky gringo who needed to be talked into landing his trout the way an air-traffic controller will talk in a novice flyer who is forced to take the controls in an emergency.

"Walk him to that bar. Don't step out too far; it drops off. Point him back toward the lake."

As Bob expertly fought the trout and brought it closer and closer, Radziwill hop-scotched in front of him, bent over, and lifted the trout by the gills. Blood spurted. The fish was a goner. My American companions were horrified, although they contained their horror until we gathered round the table to consume the delicious wild fish, its flesh pink and flavorful the way that farm-raised fish can never be.

As the wine flowed, Radziwill, who had returned home, was roundly excoriated by the holier-than-thou American anglers.

"Guys," I pointed out, "this is a European nobleman. As a matter of course, they used to do this sort of thing to people! After all, it was just a fish."

What I am saying is that catch-and-release is a great idea, a moral idea, and a sound conservation practice. But the angler who now and again takes one home to cook is not, necessarily, a barbarian. Better if it is from an unpressured stream.

And here is another life lesson: You may practice catch-and-release as a religion, but that doesn't mean the next person has to bow down to your god. As long as he or she is not a profligate trout murderer, then live and let live and stop trying to evangelize when you are out fishing. As a wise old German, Immanuel Kant, once observed, "Out of the crooked timber of humanity no straight thing was ever made."

So I hope you throw your fish back, but I will not vote to send you to trout jail for your (once) yearly plate of pan-fried fish, dredged in cornmeal and salt and crisped in bubbling brown butter in a black iron pan.

As you can see, fly fishing has its own code of conduct, but it shares much with any moral code. Earlier I said live and let live is important. This notion extends throughout the sport.

The father of modern Mexican democracy, Benito Juárez, said, *"El respeto al derecho ajeno es la paz,"* which means, "Peace lies in respecting the rights of others." This is certainly true in fishing. If you are fishing up a stream and come to someone in front of you fishing the next pool, the rule is to leave it to the person who was there first. This may be hard to do if the fish are rising all around, but it is part of the unwritten code of fly fishing.

Even more stringent, if you are fishing downstream and arrive at a pool at the same time that someone is fishing upstream, you must yield the pool because it is harder for the other angler to wade against the current than to wade with the aid of it. Similarly, if you are in a boat and there are anglers on the shore with fish between you and them, remember that it is harder for them to move than it is for you; leave the fish and go find others. Likewise, if you have traveled ten miles in your skiff to get to a bonefish flat at a certain point in the tide and, when you arrive, someone is already poling across it, stay off it. You could easily spook the fish that the other boat has so long and carefully approached.

It is all very much a fisherly version of the Golden Rule, but most conflicts in life could be settled by resorting to the timeless wisdom of simple courtesy.

The Living Planet

LIFE ALWAYS GOES ON

Fly fishing surely gives meaning to my life, but not nearly so much as life gives meaning to fly fishing. The quickening of the earth in spring means that trout will soon be on the feed. I have walked through May woods a thousand times, impatient to be at the water but always (well, almost always) mindful of the fiddlehead ferns about to unfurl, the first morels peeping up through the damp ground, the light brushstrokes of dogwood blooms seen through winter-bare branches. And of course, the warmth! Winter has been chased back to the hell where it rightfully belongs.

Casting a line and connecting to a fish is not—as the laws of physics would have it—holding on to a live electric wire. But I am not talking about physics. I am concerned instead with what goes on inside my heart when I hook up: I am lit up by a thousand watts of life.

We humans are hard-wired that way. And once the door of nature is opened, then life in all its unpredictable, rewarding, astonishing, befuddling complexity walks inside us and throws a party. At other times it writes a sonnet or dirge, but even with dirges, in the very next moment life goes on.

This was brought home to me in the beautiful (in terms of weather), heartbreaking (in terms of world events) autumn of 2001 in New York. It was the best of years and, for obvious reasons, the worst of years. I am talking not just about world events, but about our local champions in pinstripes: the striped bass.

It started at Montauk Point, Long Island. All my autumns do. Think of that spit of land as the mouth of a funnel between the mainland and the

Gulf Stream that widens north to include the waters
from the Grand Banks. In this fertile saltwater stew
there is, in the summer, life everywhere, and it ac-
counts for what is, in my opinion, the most spec-
tacular migration of wildlife on our planet, and
leading it, the great herds of striped bass that amass
close to shore in a dizzying feeding frenzy.

This year, different story. On September 9
I rounded the Point chasing albacore and looking for
bass. As we came upon the south side, there were no
anglers. Strange, I thought, as I looked on the beach
at Turtle Cove where one year ago the bass beat the
water to a froth. There were no bass in the sea, but
on the shore, three women in long black chardors,
their faces covered by veils, walked along the water's
edge, robes blowing in the wind. Seen against the
lighthouse that stood against the sky like a minaret,
it reminded me of a scene from a Bergman movie or
a Middle Eastern production of *Macbeth*.

Of course, they were just three women out for
a walk and a gab on the beach, but two days later,
when I watched the tip of Manhattan explode, the

image of those women seemed like an omen. All through that week, clear blue skies and south winds gathered the bass, but as the torrent of life prepared to move toward our city and down the coast, I am certain the cloud of death from New York rode the west winds to the Point. A week later, a vicious nor'easter—the worst in thirty years—scoured the beaches, heaved the sandbars far offshore, and sent the bass God knows where.

But life will go on, and it must keep moving no matter what madness humans unleash. The bait stayed, and where the bait stays, the fish will always come. Finally, three weeks later we fought our way through heavy seas to Caswells Point a mile west of Montauk. There were huge blitzes, miles of them: bass, albies, and blues, all mixed. I moved into the schools looking for the square tails of stripers. They were always massed in a tight, cacophonous bunch. I cast into them and hooked fish after fish.

That's the way it's supposed to be, but the en-tropy of September somehow had seeped east to Montauk, and it wasn't until this day that the natural order reasserted itself. That Sunday night, my friend Brendan McCarthy called to report that the migration had finally made its way to New York City. Big bass off Breezy Point. 'Nuff said. I picked up a roast chicken at the deli on Verandah Place and we drove out to Dead Horse Bay, hopped in Brendan's skiff, and made for the Point. In the spring, our heading would have been for the Twin Towers. Now that same course pointed to a gaping hole on the horizon. We moved into the heaving rip. The blitzes were there. Pure bass. The bad news is, whenever we motored up on them, they went down. Brendan gave in and picked up a spinning rod and fished deep. Soon he was into a thirty-inch striper.

We moved inshore to escape the wind. Brendan mounted the poling platform, and because the wind was fair and the water clear, I sent a hopeful cast to a moving shadow. A huge bass followed. I stripped and paused. He rushed my fly. I moved, and then he saw the boat and made for deep water.

There is life in these waters yet, I thought; more life than you can number. These fish will move past the harbor, millions of them will turn right and move past the place where the morning shadows of the Twin Towers last played on the waters. Pinstripe champions, New Yorkers. Eventually, even after a sad season, they will always come back—because that is what life does, and that is why I go fishing.

WORDS TO LIVE AND FISH BY

Fly fishing, though practiced by comparatively few anglers, has inspired a wealth of sporting literature. Let me correct that: Some of it is literature, the rest is as gushy as a teenager's love note. What follows are some of my favorite words by authors both famous and not so famous, but all of them wise.

"Rivers and the inhabitants of the watery elements are made for wise men to contemplate and for fools to pass by without consideration."

—IZAAK WALTON,
The Complete Angler

"In our family, there was no clear line between religion and fly fishing. We lived at the junction of great trout rivers in western Montana, and our father was a Presbyterian minister and a fly fisherman who tied his own flies and taught others. He told us about Christ's disciples being fishermen, and we were left to assume, as my brother and I did, that all first-class fishermen on the Sea of Galilee were fly fishermen and that John, the favorite, was a dry fly fisherman."

—NORMAN MACLEAN,
A River Runs through It

"There's no taking trout with dry breeches."

—MIGUEL DE CERVANTES,
Spanish writer, 1547–1616

"I fish because I love to; because I love the environs where trout are found, which are invariably beautiful, and hate the environs where crowds of people are found, which are invariably ugly; because of all the television commercials, cocktail parties, and assorted social posturing I thus escape; because, in a world where most men seem to spend their lives doing things they hate, my fishing is at once an endless source of delight and an act of small rebellion; because trout do not lie or cheat and cannot be bought or bribed or impressed by power, but respond only to quietude and humility and endless patience; because I suspect that men are going along this way for the last time, and I for one don't want to waste the trip; because mercifully there are no telephones on trout waters; because only in the woods can I find solitude without loneliness; because bourbon out of an old tin cup always tastes better out there; because maybe one day I will catch a mermaid; and, finally, not because I

regard fishing as being so terribly important but because I suspect that so many of the other concerns of men are equally unimportant—and not nearly so much fun."

—ROBERT TRAVER (AKA JUDGE JOHN VOELKER), *Trout Madness*

"The traveler fancies he has seen the country. So he has, the outside of it at least; but the angler only sees the inside. The angler only is brought close, face to face with the flower and bird and insect life of the rich river banks, the only part of the landscape where the hand of man has never interfered."

—CHARLES KINGSLEY, nineteenth-century clergyman

"An old man in his final breaths called in his family and said, 'I must apologize to you all. I suppose I haven't been the perfect father and husband. I shamefully admit that I spent as much of my life as I could in the woods and on the streams. I was rarely at home during the fishing seasons, and I'll admit that I spent too much time at the fly shop, and too much money on rods and lines and reels.' He paused here to rest for a minute, then continued. 'I've been a terrible father and I

Words to Live and Fish By

hope you all forgive me.' He paused again and looked around. Then he closed his eyes and smiled and said in a half-whisper to himself, 'On the other hand, I've caught a helluva lot of trout.' "

—ANONYMOUS

"The fisherman has a harmless, preoccupied look; he is a kind of vagrant, that nothing fears. He blends himself with the trees and the shadows. All his approaches are gentle and indirect. He times himself to the meandering, soliloquizing stream; he addresses himself to it as a lover to his mistress; he woos it and stays with it till he knows its hidden secrets. Where it deepens, his purpose deepens; where it is shallow, he is indifferent. He knows how to interpret its every glance and dimple; its beauty haunts him for days."

—JOHN BURROUGHS,
American naturalist, 1886

"The charm of fishing is that it is the pursuit of what is elusive but attainable, a perpetual series of occasions for hope."

—SIR JOHN BUCHAN,
LORD TWEEDSMUIR, Scottish writer

"To go fishing is the chance to wash one's soul with pure air, with the rush of the brook, or with the shimmer of sun on blue water. It brings meekness and inspiration from the decency of nature, charity toward tackle-makers, patience toward fish, a mockery of profits and egos, a quieting of hate, a rejoicing that you do not have to decide a darned thing until next week. And it is discipline in the equality of men—for all men are equal before fish."

—HERBERT HOOVER,
thirty-first president of the United States

"A man may fish with the worm that hath eat of a king, and eat of the fish that hath fed of that worm."

—WILLIAM SHAKESPEARE,
Hamlet, act IV, scene 3, lines 29–30

"If fishing is like religion, then fly fishing is high church."

—TOM BROKAW,
broadcast journalist and writer

"To me heaven would be a big bull ring with me holding two barrera seats and a trout stream outside that no one else was allowed to fish in and two lovely houses in the town; one

where I would have my wife and children and be
monogamous and love them truly and well and the other
where I would have my nine beautiful mistresses on nine
different floors."

—ERNEST HEMINGWAY,
American writer

"There is no fun in a thorough understanding of any subject.
A domain that naturally contains more mystery than is
solvable on any given day, like fishing, is very enjoyable.
Such mystery overflows itself."

—SCOTT BOWEN,
The Midnight Fish and Other Stories

"It's easy enough to emphasize the rituals of fly fishing, its
daily and seasonal rhythms, the languorous, almost
supplicating beat of a long casting stroke. These are some of
the things that make fly fishing a lifelong sport, a sport of
ever-deepening complexity. But those rituals and rhythms
inevitably belong to the everyday world we inhabit and they
overlay, on the stream, a world we perceive only in flashes,
when, for a moment, we're able to concentrate on the

Words to Live and Fish By

Words to Live and Fish By

swiftness, the abruptness, the almost unimaginable profusion of what nature has laid before us. It is to strengthen those moments of concentration that one goes fly fishing, and a lifetime is barely long enough to learn what they contain."

—VERLYN KLINKENBORG,
in *Trout Fisher's Almanac*

"Creeps and idiots cannot conceal themselves for long on a fishing trip."

—JOHN GIERACH,
American writer

"' The catching of fish,' said the Sage of Chocoloskee, ' is but an incident in fishing.' He told the frozen truth. To be out in the open where fish are; to watch them at their great business of living; to see them in the water or out of the water; to fish for them, and even to hook them and have them get away—all this is wonderfully worthwhile—wonderfully better worthwhile than merely more to catch and keep the stiffening fading body of one of the most beautiful forms of life."

—GIFFORD PINCHOT,
Fishing Talk

"Somebody just back of you while you are fishing is as bad as someone looking over your shoulder while you write a letter to your girl."

—ERNEST HEMINGWAY,
"Letters from Europe,"
The Toronto Star Weekly,
November 17, 1923

"The objective of advice to anglers is twofold. If they profit by it, they catch more fish. If they learn from it that enjoyment of the sport for itself is just as important, they are tasting the full flavor of the angler's reward. The frustrations of inexperience can be discouraging, the pleasure of gratification which go with intelligent practice will more than compensate. The value of experience is great, that of observation hardly less so. No one angler will ever know all there is to know about fishing. It is one of the reasons why this sport is so universally popular. To the experimental and inquiring mind, casting a fly onto the stream is one part of a never-ending study of nature."

—JOHN ATHERTON,
The Fly and the Fish

Words to Live and Fish By

"*I am not against golf, since I cannot but suspect it keeps armies of the unworthy from discovering trout.*"

—PAUL O'NEIL,
angler

"*If fishing is interfering with your business, give up your business.*"

—SPARSE GREY HACKLE
(AKA ALFRED W. MILLER),
angling author

"*Now the doctor said, ' Son, I think you ought to know
That your cholesterol's high and your IQ's low
Your beer-drinkin', good-timin' days are through
And you need trifocals and a vasectomy too.'
Gone fishin'
Gone fishin' today
Gone fishin'
Gonna fish all my troubles away.*"

—DR. THOMAS AKSTENS,
fly fisher, professor, musician

"*Scholars have long known that fishing eventually turns men into philosophers. Unfortunately, it is almost impossible to buy decent tackle on a philosopher's salary.*"

—PATRICK F. McMANUS,
American writer

"*Many go fishing all their lives without knowing that it is not fish they are after.*"

—HENRY DAVID THOREAU,
American writer

The Next Generation

**OFTEN THE BEST TEACHER
OF YOUR CHILDREN IS NOT YOU**

Most fly fishing dads hope that their offspring will share their enthusiasm for the sport. It doesn't always work out that way and even when it does, children have a way of doing things by their internal guidance system, not yours.

My eldest daughter, Lucy, is now sixteen. We have been fishing together since her third or fourth year. The first trip was in a rented dory in South Wellfleet, Massachusetts, one Labor Day. The bluefish were running all over the harbor, and I expected that they were all small ("snapper blues"). Even young Lucy could haul them in on the spinning rod that I brought and planned to cast for her. I had promised her we would fry up our catch for dinner.

The blues turned out to be quite a bit bigger, more than a young girl (or boy) could handle. I cast my fly and tied into a fierce eight-pounder. Lucy screamed with glee and purely out of high spirits sang the theme from *Pippi Longstocking*.

When the fish bit my leader off, Lucy consoled me. "That's okay, Daddy, I'll have pesto instead." Big City girl and Big City palate, I thought.

There followed trips on party boats from Sheepshead Bay, Brooklyn. Then overnight at a fly fishing camp for young girls on the Beaverkill and, when she was nine or ten, a trip to the West and Yellowstone Park, where I learned an important lesson about teaching your kid: Someone else can often do it better.

There were four of us on Lamar Creek: me, Lucy, Larry Aiuppy of Livingston, Montana, and his wife (and partner), Jan. Unlike the neighboring, more famous Slough Creek, the very fishy stretches of the Lamar run parallel to the highway and at

some distance from the road. It has been my experience that anglers will walk miles along the banks
of heavily fished streams like the Slough before
they will cross a mile of meadow to reach relatively
unfished water—maybe it has to do with being near
the sound of rushing water or the possibility of
seeing a rise. As a consequence of this predictable
angling behavior, the Lamar belonged to us.

The blue cloudless sky arched over the valley.
The sun beat down. No trout stirred. It was too
early in the season for hoppers and too late for a
midday hatch. Then heavy black clouds moved in
from the west, thunderclaps rolled across the valley,
and lightning danced around the peaks. Lucy and
Jan huddled beneath the undercut bank. I crouched
beneath some boulders. There was a double
rainbow to our east.

When the summer storm passed, the hatch
began of that most poetically named mayfly, the
Pale Morning Dun, with pastel mustard body and
clear purplish wings. As the flies took wing, the sur-

face of the stream came alive with the deliberate and prolonged rises that characterize the native trout of these western waters, the red-throated cousin of the rainbow, the cutthroat.

Jan, a graceful and powerful caster, worked with Lucy woman-to-woman. I watched from afar. Jan was doing a better job than any parent could— no parent-child static. Lucy's cast was crisp, with a tight loop. She cast into the currents at the tail of the pool. Twice she hooked a fish—the first she had ever enticed to the dry fly—but she was just a little late in setting the hook, and the fish escaped. Still, she felt some pride in an artful presentation and a take, which are the most important first steps in fly fishing. The next day on our friends' ranch, she cast the dry fly and caught a half-dozen cutts. Again, a double rainbow arched over the valley, which I am sure had something to do with her good luck.

My dream: Lucy would one day be a bona fide powerful caster and as good as any guy in catching fish.

Careful what you dream for.

We were in Argentina, on the Rio Traful in the Patagonian Andes. Sometimes—on rare windless days—its waters look as if they are not there at all. Except for a slight emerald tinge from which the Arroyo Verde, a tributary, takes its name, the river is as clear as mountain air.

Our guide, Martin Sere, could have passed for ten years younger than his fifty-four, thanks to a life in the outdoors, guiding for trout and deer in the temperate months and skiing in cold weather. He was an eager and patient teacher for Lucy.

On our first morning, he took her to a pool known as the Tranquera (I looked in the book at the lodge: Ernie Schwiebert had caught a trout of three kilos—seven-and-a-half pounds—there). They left me in midpool to fish the dry fly while Martin worked on Lucy's roll cast with a wet.

I cast across the stream to a pocket below some green lilylike plants. The red shoulders of a large brown trout seized my gaze as its mouth closed on my fly. The tug was strong and violent. I

struck back as it tore first downstream, then up then
down again. As I tried to turn it, Martin yelled, "Let
it run!" but I was too late, and my rod sprung back
when the trout broke free.

"Damn it," I repeated no less than four times.

"That's okay, Dad," Lucy consoled as she had
when she was four. "There are plenty more. I caught
two like that."

This would not be the first time in the course
of our week that Lucy would outfish me. As she
caught big fish and learned to play them, her confidence increased and her casting improved, thanks
in no small part to her guide. The mystique of a for-
eign place and the daily life in our enchanted valley
made it more than fly fishing boot camp—and that
helped too.

Lunchtimes we would repair to the lodge, an
elegant chalet presided over by Maurice Lariviere,
a debonair Argentine gent. Holding forth over a
bottle of good wine and sumptuous grass-fed beef,
he seemed to have stepped out of a Patagonian version of a Fred Astaire movie. The table talk was al-

ways about fish, horses, Ben Hogan's putt in the 1948 Open, Lester Young's sax solo on *Lush Life*. It was never about business—that would have been bad form.

By our final day, we were ready to try something new, so we drove two hours out of the verdant Traful valley back to the sere high Patagonia desert along the valley of the Collon Cura. A herd of guanacos—like super svelte llama—grazed in the lowlands. A large eagle perched on top of a thirty-foot roadside crucifix.

"Powerful symbol," Lucy said, and I agreed.

Finally we reached the Alumine. Wide and clear, bordered by willows, a symphony of a stream in comparison to the chamber orchestra of the Traful.

I went upstream. Lucy and Martin descended to the chute at the end of a riffle. I stuck with the dry fly. Lucy fished a wet. The wind was up and quartering over her casting shoulder. Though normally a nuisance, it occurred to me that this was good because Martin had taught her how to face away from the wind and to double-haul her back-cast into it.

I kept moving upstream to a pool I have successfully fished before. It should have been a whole lot better than it was. Somewhat dispirited, I returned to our van. Lucy, already de-wadered, was doing her Latin homework. (She made a deal with her school to get the week off: "Go fish," they encouraged, "but do your *Aeneid*.") She wore wildflowers in her hair. "How many did you get?" she asked.

"A few," I said unenthusiastically and hoped to leave it at that.

She wouldn't let me off gracefully. "Well, how many?"

"Three," I kind of fibbed.

"How big?" she pressed.

"I don't remember."

"Yes you do," she bore down.

"Okay," I fibbed again. "The biggest was twelve inches."

Martin looked up and said, *"Si tú crias cuervos te van a comer los ojos,"* which means, "If you raise crows they will eat your eyes." It seemed both true and not so bothersome because I was happy that my young "crow" had finally moved into the class of real fly fisherpeople. It is a sport that can carry her through a lifetime, and that is the most important thing.

Getting Older

ASKING FOR HELP IS A SIGN

OF MATURITY, NOT AGE

In a fly fisher's memory, it is always late spring, nothing hurts when you cast, and you can still see clearly enough to tie on the smallest fly. That is the great consolation of memory when, as it must, we get older, and the step into the stream at fifty is an oafish imitation of the nimble jump of the twenty-year-old. Your shoulder hurts when you cast; you need magnifying glasses to thread your fly. So what? I have known anglers who fished, and fished well, into their eighties.

The key to enjoyment at fifty-five is the same as the key to enjoyment at fifteen: Do whatever you

can do as well as you can, then try to do a little
more—but don't try to rewrite the record books. You
probably can't, and it's not important anyway. No
one, or at least no true angler, keeps score. There is
no score, only the moment and the next fish.

I knew that Father Time was catching up with
me—and damned near overtook me—one September afternoon on the jetty at Breezy Point, the
easternmost arm of the long crescent of Gateway
National Park that forms the Lower Bay of New
York Harbor.

The wind was from the southwest and the tide
was rising. Low-wheeling bands of gulls occasionally dipped to the water, and beneath them were
tell-tale white slashes. My heart swelled as we saw
leaping albacore. The albacore, or more properly,
false albacore, is perhaps the most exciting game
fish for the surf angler. He is big, fast, strong, and
dogged. I think of him as the fishing version of the
grouse: You must be prepared at all times for your
quarry to make a lighting fast appearance, and when
he does, you must guess his direction and then re-

spond quickly and accurately if you hope to inter-
cept his path.

At the end of the jetty we saw a number of fly
casters fighting fish. For years I have made my way
to the end of the jetty even though it is, in my
opinion, a booby trap put there by the Department
of Public Works. About twenty yards from the end
(in other words, right where the fish are), there are
two rocks separated by a six-foot gap. Going from
one to the other requires a jump then a forward lean
to grab the top of the rock just landed on.

I leapt and took a good, shoulder-crunching
fall. The waves washed over me, but I held onto the
rock with my right arm and pulled myself up. I was
soaked, cold, and—in regard to jetty jumping—
finished. I righted myself and began to cast, hoping
that the fish would come within range. They didn't.
Meanwhile, Peter Chan, a devout Breezyphile who
works at Urban Angler in Manhattan, was standing
at the tip of the jetty catching fish after fish. There
was nothing I could do but watch the show and get
vicarious pleasure from my friend's success.

I knew then and there that my years of hopping to the end of the jetty were over.

Now consider wading. Mastering the physics of moving and turning a human body in flowing water over rocky, slippery river bottom is an art. It also requires strength and balance, two qualities that tend to come down a notch or two as we get older.

My latest adventure in wading started when we drove down an old logging road to the wildest stretch of the West Branch of the Ausable. My two companions were my longtime fishing partner, Tom Akstens of Baker's Mills, New York, and Fritz Mitchell of Charlotte, Vermont. The air was wet with a passing rain, and the understory of the forest was a thicket of aspen, wildflowers, and pale green caribou moss. The leaves dripped with heavy summer mist, and mosquitoes feasted on all warm-blooded creatures. In the late golden sun, the Tinker Bell flutter of mayfly wings filled the air with sparkling light.

The water was high. The wading was a bear. Fritz, who prefers to fish rough pocket water, spotted the broad shoulders of a rising fish. He directed me to the best place to cast across the complex current. I leaned on my wading staff and fought my way out. I cast. The fish rose. My fly dragged. The fish went down. I presented my fly again. He rose again but, on subsequent casts, declined to reappear.

With that, Fritz said we should move to the next good trout lie upstream. I turned in the current and inched my way toward shore. The river nudged me downstream. When I lifted my foot, it was like stepping off a ledge. As I tried to catch a foothold, I knew what was coming. There is a disquieting, *oh damn!* inevitability to that split second between the moment you know you have stepped too far into a swift current and the moment it overflows your waders. You have a clear sense of having reached the tipping point, a feeling of the world slowing down as it does before a traffic crash. And there's nothing you can do about it except get wet.

I didn't have enough purchase on the bottom to move backward. I had to move forward at all

costs. I tippy-toed until I was on point like a ballerina and then ran out of toe room. The water lapped
over the top of my waders and filled my boots. I re-
coiled from the shock and pressed on to the bank.
But that was just bad luck and had nothing to do
with age.

Wet, but determined to get even with the
trout, I moved on. We forded at a nonsuicidal spot
and entered the water below the outlet of a feeder
creek.

Fritz waded into the pocket water with the
ease of a rhino walking through tall grass. He tied
on a Gray Wulff and—bam, bam, bam, bam—took
four nice brook trout. He advised me to cast near
some rocks and to pass by others. Every rock that
he thought would yield a trout did: all lovely
brookies.

"If you are up for it," he suggested, "the flat
rock below the pool takes some wading, but I know
there's a nice fish there."

"No way," I said faintheartedly.

"You're doing it," he commanded.

I fought through the current, bird-dogging Fritz's footsteps. I reached a point where I knew I could not manage the current, so Fritz and I locked arms to form a more stable wading profile. Knowing you need help and then not feeling unmanned about requesting it may mean you are admitting your age, but the point is to catch fish, isn't it?

Fritz led me to a spot where there was enough gravel to dig in and plant myself. He gave me a Stimulator, a good pocket water pattern that imitates a large stonefly. Per his instructions, I laid out a long cast and threw an upstream mend when it hit the water. The fly floated through a slick and then past the trunk of a deadfall against the far bank.

Nothing.

I cast again. The fly spun in the eddy. Just at the point where the line was going to begin to drag, a large fat rainbow slammed it and, in the same motion, launched itself a foot into the air.

Tom whooped with excitement. Fritz too. He counseled me to edge my way backward to the bank and then to fight the fish as I followed downstream.

No way. I would beat the fish where I stood or I would lose him, but I wasn't going to take another dunking.

The rainbow proved pugnacious but compliant. Within minutes I had him in my hands. He was the best fish and certainly the most dramatic one of my trip. Being cold and wet and needing some assistance in wading was, at that moment, very beside the point, so I asked Fritz to help me back.

I guess the lesson at fifty-five is the same as the one that my mom tried to instill in me in my more rambunctious, youthful moments: Act your age.

A FLY FISHER'S HEROES

There are many anglers—some famous, some unfamous, some downright anonymous, some living, some now gone— who have taught me something about how to fish and, more important, how to think and feel about our mutual love: fly fishing.

GENE CALOGERO

My first mentor. I met him on the Esopus Creek in 1974. He was catching lots of fish; I was catching a few. We struck up a conversation. Small world: It turned out his cabin was right across the street from mine on the Little Beaverkill in Mt. Tremper, New York.

Gene was an art director at Gray Advertising on the Mustang account. He was a Bronx-born Italian-American. When we first became friends, he had sworn off the dry fly. It wasn't a matter of principle; it was more of an intellectual challenge. Gene was well aware that trout eat many more nymphs, or immature mayflies, than duns, or mature flies. He had bought Ernest Schwiebert's masterful work *Nymphs*, and his artist's eye found it somewhat wanting. No surprise: There is no such thing as a one-size-fits-all fly-tying manual. Mayfly nymphs may vary in size or color from place to place. So working from Schwiebert's foundation, he had set himself the task of tying a series of nymphs that reflected the aquatic life in our stream. He was off the dry fly until he completed his task, which he never did.

Gene, a cancer survivor, eventually succumbed to a heart attack, but he had ten great years of fishing, and I had ten years of companionship and tutelage in fly tying. He also taught me how to mix a perfect Rob Roy, which I can recommend as one of the two or three greatest postfishing cocktails.

JOHN VOELKER

Most of the world knew him by his pen name, Robert Traver, but I knew him by his given name, John Voelker. A small town D. A. in the remote U. P. (Upper Peninsula of Michigan), he saw the very best, but more often the worst, of humanity. One such case led him to write the book *Anatomy of a Murder*, which became a national bestseller. Otto Preminger made a movie of it starring Jimmy Stewart and paid John one million dollars for the rights—a nice paycheck these days, but a fortune back then.

At that time John was a justice of the Michigan Supreme Court, in which capacity he wrote one of the classic opinions in American jurisprudence—"the Great Skinny Dipping Case." A group of young people had been arrested for offending public decency by taking off their clothes and jumping into a local swimming hole. "Private nudity is no offense to public decency," John wrote, and his ruling stands to this day.

When John cashed his movie check, he said, "That's it. I have enough money. For the rest of my life I am going to fish." And that's what he did: for gorgeous native brook trout that lived in the beaver ponds on his boggy property in the U. P. You would find John there every day, fishing or playing pinochle with his buddies—and for sure at one time or another, he would drink a bourbon old-fashioned. Not any old bourbon, mind you, but cheap bourbon. John had no need for the fancy stuff. Oh yes, he was also one of the greatest angling writers the sport of fly fishing has ever produced.

JACK ALLEN

The Danish philosopher Søren Kierkegaard said, "Purity of Heart is to will one thing." Jack Allen is the purest fisherman I know. He fishes for largemouth bass with a popping bug in the Everglades. Trout and salmon fishermen and hunters of the bonefish and tarpon may find it strange that I hold in highest regard a guy who fishes the way they fished in farm ponds and lazy Ozark rivers a half-century ago, but Jack knows what he likes—and what he likes is the explosion on the surface when a largemouth engulfs a popping bug delivered on a fly.

He also likes the solitude of the watery prairie that the Seminole Indians called the River of Grass. In his small johnboat, outfitted with two swivel seats and Astroturf, Jack has the company of alligators, herons, flamingoes, sawgrass, and the ever-rolling sky all to himself. He fishes light rods and heavy lines—an anathema to gear heads—but it allows him to pick up his line, make one false cast, and shoot his bug up against a coral bank from which it will fall, and the sound of it hitting the water will summon a bass. Jack is a lifelong bebop fan, and he drives an old van. In fifty years in the Glades he has never come across one instance where he has needed a four-wheel drive, and he fishes where only alligators and old Indians go—which tells you something about how necessary it is to have an SUV to drive to the supermarket parking lot.

When he is not guiding for bass in the south, Jack goes north to fish for smallmouth. In the phone book he is listed as Jack Bass Allen. Like I said, he knows what he likes, and he has devoted his life to it.

BEN MONTANELLI

Chances are, you never heard of Ben Montanelli. He is not a fishing celebrity. But he is the most naturally talented trout fisherman I ever met. Like me, he was a little aimless and a little hippie-ish back in the late 1970s—except for the laserlike focus that trout fishing gave to his life. I am a better caster than Ben, and that, many would have you believe, is ninety percent of the game. Not so. Ben proved his angling superiority in sunny weather and foul, in the high water of early spring and the low water of fall, with huge stonefly nymphs fished on lead weight droppers and teeny Griffiths Gnats the size of a rosebud.

I think Ben's great talent is that he watches and listens. Rather than approaching a stream with a fixed idea, he came at each fishing session with the notion that he would see what the trout were up to and adjust his tactics, his flies, his cast. He would wade thirty yards up a quiet pool on the East Branch of the Delaware, taking twenty minutes to get there so that he made the barest ripple and therefore avoided spooking any trout between his point of entry and his target. When he was close enough to make an accurate cast with a light touch, he would stop and look for little microcurrents, floating ants, or grasshoppers. Finally, when he decided what the trout wanted and how they wanted it, he would cast. Result: Ben caught many fish on few casts, and I caught some fish on a lot of long casts. Take your time, watch, and listen—that's Ben.

LARRY AIUPPY

They call him "the stomach that walks like a man" because he can eat you out of house and home in one sitting. At six-foot-four, with the build of an NFL fullback, "delicate" is not the first word that comes to mind when you see Larry. When he sports a beard, he looks like the mountain man that he was when he led survival trips for Outward Bound. A native of Pittsburgh and a college graduate with a major in deep German philosophy, he took a trip to Yellowstone Park that convinced him to move to Livingston, Montana.

He had already established himself in the world of high-priced fashion photography in New York but easily made the change to western and wildlife scenes—make that Americana in general. For our wedding, he gave my wife and I a picture of a bison, thigh-deep in a snowdrift in Yellowstone Park, his shaggy mane covered with white flakes. When Larry wades the powerful currents of the Yellowstone, he reminds me of that bison. He bulls his away across a current that would knock me over. But it is not power that I learned from Larry; rather, it is the sense of what he calls the Completed Act.

We were on one of the spring creeks in Paradise Valley, Montana; by its appearance, well-named. I had cast to and hooked the biggest brown trout of my life. I was quite impressed because he had taken a small fly on light leader, one that I had reasoned he would find irresistible. It didn't bother me that he broke off after two leaps. Larry, on the other hand, was less impressed, explaining, "The Completed Act is to present the right fly, to have the fish strike, to subdue it, and not allow it to take you under rocks and branches where it can break free, to bring it to hand, to land it, to revive it, and to watch it swim away. Anything less doesn't count." In other words, there is no such thing as good enough to Larry Aiuppy: A fish is well-caught or it isn't.

LEE WULFF

Having fished with Lee Wulff; having watched him tie flies; having walked with him through autumn woods, shotgun in hand, stalking grouse; having flown over the valley of the Beaverkill with him at the controls of the small plane in which he later crashed and died, I feel like a baseball player who can say he took batting lessons with Joe DiMaggio or a clarinetist who had Benny Goodman over for a jam session. By general acclamation, Lee was the most influential fly fisher of the twentieth century. He invented the Wulff series of flies (dry flies with a deer-hair wing that gives them supreme floatability). He made the first fishing vest by sewing the pockets from a pair of Levi's onto a vest that he bought at Bloomingdale's. Lee made a fly line with exactly the reverse physics of any fly line I ever saw (it was light in front, heavy in back). He thought the object of the game was to take the biggest fish on the lightest tackle in the shortest time—and he could do it!

I have always been inspired by the way Lee became a full-time fly fisherman. As a young artist, he went to Paris in the 1920s, the same time that Hemingway, Fitzgerald, and the rest of the Lost Generation were sipping absinthe, hanging out with Picasso, and generally becoming famous together. Not Lee—at least not yet. He returned to the States and took a job with DuPont as a package designer.

As the country plunged into the Depression, Lee was sitting pretty with a well-paying job, but then a friend was fired two months before his sixty-fifth birthday and retirement. "Right then and there," Lee remembered, "I decided I would never compete for money again." Lee quit his job. He spent that summer, 1932, camping and fishing with Dan Bailey in the Catskills, and he tied his first Wulff flies on the banks of the Esopus. He never looked back. He guided, lectured, wrote, taught. Some years were flush, some not-so-flush. We are all his kids in what he called "this wonderful sport."

A. J. McCLANE

Al McClane's writing is so clear it is almost invisible. He just tells the story, and it is as if it is your thoughts you are hearing rather than his words. Born in Brooklyn, he went to agricultural school upstate and fished the same Catskill streams that I fished two generations later.

In terms of seeing the world and experiencing all the fishing there was to be had, he was probably the most complete angler who ever lived. On every continent with every kind of tackle, he brought the world within reach of every angler, or at least within reach of the daydreams of every angler. If you were to ask me to choose one person as my role model, it would be Al. He wrote about fishing and food, my two passions, and he also proved to me that you can make your passion into your livelihood—if you are willing to play a little chicken with fate. In the late fifties, Al was the fishing editor of *Field & Stream* and the best-known fishing journalist alive. He decided to chuck it all and move down to Palm Beach, Florida, where he could fish largemouth in the Glades and be close to the bonefishing of the Keys and the Bahamas.

At that same time, Holt, Rinehart, and Winston bought *Field & Stream*, largely because Al was one of its crown jewels. They were panicked when they found out their star player had quit the team. They offered him a pile of money to come back to New York, but Al was through with the Big City. "Okay," the new owners said. "If we can keep your name on the masthead, we will pay you the same salary we just offered and you stay in Palm Beach." Al accepted and went from no job to the best job in the business.

PAUL DIXON

I have fly fished the East End of Long Island for sixteen years. When I first started there, we basically did what the conventional tackle fishermen did: We went at dawn and dusk; we fished around jetties and rips; we looked for feeding gulls. Paul Dixon, a fair-haired California boy, ran the fishing department at the Orvis store in New York. A few years later, Paul moved out to the East End of Long Island and opened up a guiding business and fly fishing store.

He started out fishing the traditional times and the traditional places. One afternoon, someone came into his store and told him that while standing on the cliffs overlooking the clear waters of Gardiner's Bay, he saw hundreds, perhaps thousands, of stripers cruising over the white sandy bottom. Paul made straight for the cliffs overlooking Barnes Landing and confirmed the report.

Next day, at the same point in the tide, he took his skiff to the tidal flat below the cliffs and cast to feeding stripers, the same way that one hunts bonefish or tarpon in the Florida Keys. In so doing he discovered a new way of fly fishing for stripers that has revolutionized saltwater fly fishing in the Northeast and has been responsible for the greatest growth in the sport in the last fifty years.

There were other guides in Cape Cod, Rhode Island,

and Martha's Vineyard who made a similar discovery at the same time, but Paul is the one who revealed it to me. Since that time, he has established himself as the preeminent fly rod guide at Montauk Point, one of the richest fishing grounds on earth. Go out there any day and you will notice that when Paul's boat moves, the other guides follow. As my fishing partner Josh Feigenbaum puts it, "Dixon sees it in 3-D." Paul understands the interplay of tides and bait better than anyone I have met. "The fish will be where the bait is," he says, "No bait, no fish." Simple enough, but you would be surprised at how many people flail fruitlessly at the water because the fish were there yesterday.

His other great, seemingly self-evident dictum is, "Good fishing is a function of time on the water." In other words, you have to put in lots of hours, mucho time, in order to improve as an angler and, of equal importance, in order to have any chance of truly great fishing. Remember what I said about three for ten being great in baseball? It is in any sport. In baseball, you need the at-bats; in fishing, the time on the water.

A Fly Fisher's Heroes

AL CAUCCI

Ask any trout fisher what has been the biggest advance in fly tying in recent years, and he or she will tell you "the Comparadun," or at least they *should* tell you that. It was the invention of Al Caucci and his partner Bob Nastasi. Al, a football-playing street kid from Bristol, Pennsylvania, worked his way through high school as stick man raking in the dice and the money in a roving crap game in Bristol.

But he was made for bigger things: He became a mechanical engineer and somewhere in his twenties discovered fly fishing. As it did with me, it became his ruling passion. He spent the better part of three years with a snorkel on the bottom of a trout stream studying what it is that insects do to trigger feeding among trout. The result was his book, *Hatches*, and his series of low-profile flies, the Comparadun series. Simple and elegant, they seduce the most selective trout in difficult waters.

Al is also a stickler about gear. He has taught me to always buy the best gear that you can afford. "After age fifty," he will say whenever given a chance, "it is all about the equipment." Better rods, better reels, and better lines lead to better casts, more effective fights, and more satisfying fishing. Al's combination of persistence, passion, and precision add up to a total angler.

NICK LYONS

Every religion needs its St. Paul, the spreader of the creed, the great communicator. In modern times, the lyrical writings of this gentle but rigorously logical angler and writer have been the mark against which all others are measured. He enjoys helping writers (myself included) as much as he enjoys fishing.

His prose is simple but refined. His remarkable volume *Spring Creek* is the closest thing I know to a trout-fishing haiku. As a professor of English at Hunter College in New York, he honed a knowledge of Shakespeare and the classics, which served him well as an angling writer. His "Seasonable Angler" column in *Fly Fisherman* magazine put the sport in perspective and communicated its beauty and irresistible attraction to a whole generation of which I count myself a grateful member.

Lifetime Learning

**IT IS NEVER TOO LATE TO
TEACH OLD FISHERMEN NEW TRICKS**

Have you ever heard the expression "He's a good club golfer" or "She's a good club tennis player"? Although there is no such term as a good club fly fisher, the idea still holds true. Many anglers take a few lessons when they start, then play a lot and reach a certain level, and it stops there.

This was certainly my story. I took three days of lessons from Doug Swisher on the Beaverkill in 1974 then practiced my heart out for a few years. Fishing all the while, I reached a certain level of proficiency. A guide would give me a tip now and then, but for the most part I stayed at the same level. Good, not great. In baseball terms, a good triple-A fastball but not quite major league.

Then last year I spent six weeks fishing every day. That went a long way to improving my skills. Spending a big block of time will do more for you than spending even more time broken up into haphazard chunks.

Still, I wasn't making megaleaps in my proficiency or style. Then I invited Mark Sedotti, the best caster I know, to spend a few days at my place. One afternoon off Montauk, the fishing slowed and the seas started to heave with that angry look that sends me heading for port. Meanwhile, watching Mark sit down and cast the whole fly line impressed me so much that I asked him if he would give me a casting lesson.

Back within the protecting arm of Montauk Harbor, bathed in golden light, we were sheltered from the swells and the wind that we had left on the south shore.

"Let me see you cast," he said.

I threw about fifty feet of line.

"Not bad, but we can make it better," he said. "Think of the line as an extension of the rod, because when you get up enough speed it acts that way. Then think about bending that rod all the way down to the handle and then unbending it as you release your forward cast."

Such mental pictures can often help in mastering a skill. I remember doing a story about Charlie Lau, the great batting coach of the 1970s and 1980s. Working with the Yankees of the Reggie Jackson era, he would stand behind the batting cage and constantly advise the hitters, "Think the ball up the middle." It was his opinion that this mental image produced a more balanced stroke. "If you think it up the middle, the home runs will come," he assured.

Likewise, I found that thinking about bending and unbending the whole rod kept my motion fluid and continuous and slowed it down, allowing the rod, rather than my arm, to do the work of throwing the line. Makes sense. A fishing rod is *designed* to throw line.

My casting improved more in that next week than it had it the previous twenty years.

Another golden opportunity to improve my form came on a trip to the Florida Keys in January with my friend and guide Allan Finkelman, a superb saltwater caster. Allan's stroke is bafflingly slow, yet with what looks like no effort, or very little effort, the line goes very far in a tight loop, no matter what the wind is doing.

So, one morning when the bonefishing had declined from little to none—it tends to do that in January, but I keep going at that time because I am able to, so why not?—I stood on the bow and fired off a few casts.

Allan watched and commented, "You are using way too much energy." He came forward and took my rod.

"Never confuse arm speed with line speed. A lot of physics happens between the time you move your hand and when the fly hits the water. You will be surprised how little energy you need to expend to move a lot of line accurately. Here's what I do to see how much power is needed to get the rod working optimally."

He stripped sixty feet of line from the rod and began to cast.

"I cast as lightly as I can. If all the line goes out and it pulls against the reel at the end, that means I have power in reserve. So I cast again, more lightly this time. Again, same drill. If there is reserve power, I lighten up more. I keep doing this until the cast dies. Then I add a little bit more power in, and that's what the rod requires. No need to do more—it will actually work against the efficiency of your rod, not to mention the arm fatigue factor."

Over the next few days, whenever I felt myself working hard I went back to Allan's advice. Not only did it lengthen my cast and leave me less tired, it also slowed down the cast. And slow is good.

Are you ever too old to learn? Not that I have seen. I was given eloquent proof of this one night on Silver Creek in Idaho. This famed spring creek was a favorite of Ernest Hemingway, Clark Gable, Gary Cooper, and legions of fly-rodders not quite so famous but no less passionate about their sport.

It was getting on to twilight, happy hour for the fly fisher and the trout—or at least those who avoided getting caught in their dusk feeding binge.

We were fishing a large slough, a wide, pondlike part of the stream. In order to get where the trout were we needed float tubes, which are inner tubes with a seat inside that you stick your legs through.

As we labored into our ungainly crafts, I noticed an older gent taking his time walking to the shoreline. Clearly he had lost some spring in his step. Then I recognized him: Harry Wilson, one of the pioneer graphite fly rod builders who made the Scott series of rods. They were the highest performance rods in the world at the time.

"You need a belly boat to get to the fish, Harry," I said.

"Never tried one."

I didn't think that was a big problem. "They're easy; I have another one in the truck."

Harry was game. I gave him a brief lesson in the no-brainer dos and don'ts of the belly boat, and he took a good five minutes haltingly getting in and more haltingly getting down to the water. He was the perfect image of a feeble, if willing, oldster.

But when he was afloat, everything changed. As the tube floated, Harry didn't have to worry about planting his feet on firm ground or keeping his balance as he waded. He floated like Moses in the cradle, riding the breeze and the current. Then, when he picked up his rod, all notions of aged feebleness were banished. Two false casts, a double haul, and the line shot out like a tracer bullet.

We all caught fish that night, but Harry caught the most.

Learning, you see, is a lifetime thing. You can always improve your craft, and there is always someone who is better than you to show you how. The improvement may not be immediately apparent because sometimes you have already learned to do the wrong thing and to compensate enough to perform at a high level. But in the end, good technique will improve your results.

One other lesson that seems to be a law of nature, or at least of art, as Allan's light-as-you-can trick proves again: Less, very often, is more.

Humility

DON'T BELIEVE YOUR FANS . . .

OR YOUR CRITICS

I once had a magazine assignment to cover the Dodgers' spring training in Florida. I was interviewing the owner, Peter O'Malley, a very forthcoming host (especially over one of his powerhouse Negroni's, a potent mixture of gin, vermouth, and campari tempered by a slice of orange). The Dodgers had won the World Series the previous autumn but so far had not congealed that spring.

"One thing I have learned in this business," O'Malley opined, "you are never as good as your fans say you are and never as bad as your critics would have the world believe. Just look at the job, and do it the best you can."

Flash-forward to a stream in Montana that I'll call Kitty Creek—not its name, but the rancher who owns it let me fish it with the understanding that I would not publicize it. My companions were Doug McClelland, who teaches business law at Montana State University and is a former president of Trout Unlimited, and Larry Aiuppy.

Having been warned to keep an eye out for the rattlesnakes that had come down from the parched hills, we fished the smaller upper reaches of the Kitty. My go-to fly, an Ausable Wulff, produced three or four little trout. At that point, Doug returned from an upper pool and advised me to put on a hopper. I did and instantly caught a half-dozen rainbows. The biggest was sixteen inches and the smallest not much smaller. For the next hour I experienced glorious Montana fishing that included two very fat brown trout of fifteen and seventeen inches.

"Piece of cake," I thought. "When you know what you are doing and do it well, trout are not so hard."

But pride goeth before a fall.

Having caught our fill on Kitty Creek, we made our way to the challenging (and public) tail waters of the Missouri. A half a mile in width, it is the most prolific trout water I have ever seen on three continents. When we arrived, the placid river was alive with impressive rises to teeny flies. The fish were fat as footballs and, apparently, insatiable.

Full of the confidence born of my afternoon's success, I waded in. Larry, Doug, and I—with a hundred years of collective fly rod experience—cast a thousand times to feeding fish, and we each succeeded in hooking, but *not landing*, one fish. These fish were a humbling counterpoint to the willing ingenues of the ranch streams.

Did it mean that we went from hero to zero in three hours? Not really. What it did mean, though, is that when things are going well, give thanks for your good luck, but don't confuse it with superior skill or virtue. In fishing, as in all things, there are good days and bad days, and sometimes they happen on the same day. Beware of the swelled head or the equally unproductive self-lacerating depression. Just fish as well as you can.

A Fly Fisher's
Essential Reading

Fly fishing, for reasons I don't fully understand, produces
more writing than any other kind of fishing. In fact, if you
consider how few fly fishers there are compared to golfers,
horse enthusiasts, or baseball fans, I think that proportionately
it is the most written-about sport. It is also generally
acknowledged to have more of the best sports writing, which
is not to say that it is all great. There are plenty of bloviating
gasbags out there who look at fly fishing as a way to write
overblown, over-serious, over-precious stuff. Still, there is
great writing about this sport, much more than these ten
books, but put me on a desert island—with a trout stream,
a bass pond, and a bonefish flat—and these are the books
I'd want.

IN OUR TIME
BY ERNEST HEMINGWAY

Hemingway loved to fish more than anything. When he
discovered that he could get to the marlin fishing with two
hours less traveling time if he lived in Cuba rather than Key
West, he moved to Cuba. The man had his priorities right

when it came to fishing, and it is all there in crystal clear—make that diamond bright—prose in this volume. Often imitated, never surpassed, Hemingway created a character, the returning war veteran Nick Adams, whose thoughts you would swear are your own. Without question, "Big Two-Hearted River" was the most influential fishing story of the twentieth century, perhaps of any century.

TROUT MADNESS
BY ROBERT TRAVER

I often wonder if it is coincidence that both Traver and Hemingway wrote about and fished in the Upper Peninsula of Michigan: the long flat landscape, the pine forests, the fields full of berries and wild mushrooms, and streams where trout lay in the tannic waters. Traver's *Trout Madness*, like many great works, shows that you can learn a lot staying in one place. His wry, elegant, and gentle prose prove it is not how far you travel, but how deeply you understand a place, its people, and its wild things, that are the measure of wisdom.

A RIVER RUNS THROUGH IT
BY NORMAN MACLEAN

He spent his youth fighting fires and fishing the streams
of frontier Montana. Then he became a college professor.
His courses in Shakespeare at the University of Chicago
were the perennial favorites of students for thirty years.
When I first read this slim volume in the late seventies,
I put it down and said "Wow!" It is a story of fishing to
be sure, but also of values, of brotherhood, tragedy,
and fate. I guess a lifetime of Shakespeare will do that
to you.

TARPON QUEST
BY JOHN N. COLE

I could well have chosen Cole's more famous work, *Striper*,
which is an elegiac consideration of the premier gamefish of
the Northeast. But there is something chivalric, almost a Holy
Grail quest, about Cole's late-life love affair with the sleek
silver giants of the Florida Keys. To discover something in late
middle age and to pursue it with the ardor of a young lover

has, in this case, produced a work of romance, action, even suspense, and it shows that it is not so much what you fish for, but how and why you pursue it, that brings the spiritual rewards of fly fishing.

FLY FISHING THROUGH THE MIDLIFE CRISIS
BY HOWELL RAINES

Everyone has a midlife crisis, at least everyone I know. Fly fishing got me through mine. It did the same for Howell Raines, the editor of the *New York Times*, only he had the heart and brains to write a book about it. Funny, wise, urbane, seasoned with the right amount of just-folks Southernism, it is a fine way to get to know a man, his sport, and why each was made for the other.

SUPERIOR FISHING
BY ROBERT B. ROOSEVELT

One of the pioneers of American conservation, he reestablished the shad in the Hudson and brought the

rainbow trout to the East Coast and the striped bass to
the West. He further introduced his nephew, Theodore, to
the outdoors and the conservation ethic. (He was also
considered a black sheep in the family because he happened
to have two wives and two sets of kids on the same block
in Manhattan!) In this engaging journal, Roosevelt recounts
a journey up the Mississippi to Lake Superior in the early
days of the Civil War in the company of a French nobleman
who was possibly the most dunderheaded upper-class
character in literature until P. G. Wodehouse invented Bertie
Wooster.

SPRING CREEK
BY NICK LYONS

In the 1980s, the author of "The Seasonable Angler" on the
back page of *Fly Fisherman* magazine spent three weeks on
O'Dells spring creek in Montana. The fishing was superb, and
Nick's reflections on nature, fish, fishing, and life make for a
true jewel of a volume, proving that it isn't how much you
write but how well.

HATCHES
BY AL CAUCCI AND BOB NASTASI

The twentieth century produced a series of works about mayflies and trout streams. Preston Jennings (*Book of Trout Flies*), Art Flick (*New Streamside Guide*), and Ernie Schwiebert (*Matching the Hatch*) all catalogued the sequence of mayfly hatches and the theory of flies to match them. Caucci and Nastasi's three-year pilgrimage around America and the resulting encyclopedia of flies and their Comparadun series of imitations represent the pinnacle of this tradition of passionate amateurs.

THE FLY AND THE FISH
BY JOHN ATHERTON

Atherton was a painter, a graphic artist in the advertising business, and an avid fly fisher. His lucid, colorful writing delivers an important message about the properties of light and its effects on the flies we tie to lure trout. Essentially, this is pointillism for fly fishers. Much has been written about imitation in fly tying, but nothing so expertly nor clearly as this volume. It all takes place in the milieu of genteel fly fishing, the New York Anglers Club, the Miramichi River— places and scenes not experienced by most regular folk, but charming nonetheless.

FISHING WITH McCLANE
BY A. J. McCLANE

Any book by Al McClane is worth a whole shelf's load by most other angling authors. His authority, breadth of experience with all kinds of fly fishing everywhere in the world, and his clarity of expression are the standard to which all writers should aspire.

Dare to Listen

**ACCEPTING ADVICE MAKES YOU
NO LESS A FISHERMAN (OR A MAN)**

If you are married and a male, no doubt you've lost your way en route to a new destination. So you turned around and backtracked, made a few lefts, a few rights, and so on. Equally without doubt, your exasperated mate turned to you and said, "For Pete's sake, why don't you ask somebody for directions? What is it with guys and directions? Does it emasculate you?"

I don't think emasculation is the problem. Nonetheless, the wife does have a point. Guys have a thing about asking for directions.

Do not let this trait spill over into your fishing.

If you are going to new water or trying for new kinds of fish, hire a guide. They may be expensive—hundreds of dollars a day for a top guide—but look at it this way: You work all year dreaming about a fishing trip. You pay hard-earned money for your plane ticket, your gear, maybe a rental car, a motel. So ask yourself, Will you be happier if you save a few hundred bucks and don't catch fish, or would you prefer to reach into your pocket again and get into some serious fishing?

Go ahead, Big Spender. Think of the variables in fishing that the locals know and you don't. If one stream is muddy, where is there likely to be a clear one? If the tide moves at three o'clock, where is the first place the bait will come? A guide will know the water and the fish like the back of his or her hand (more and more there are top-notch female fly rod guides).

During one trip to Argentina after a seventy-day drought, the skies poured, trying to make up for lost time. The rivers swelled, turned to chocolate, and overran their banks. On that very day that I spoke of earlier when Bob White caught his big brown on the Chimehuin, the one that Charlie Radziwill "helped" him to land, we ran into a group of do-it-yourself anglers who shivered in front of the fireplace and looked about ready to cry.

We had just come from some of the most dramatic and successful dry fly fishing I have ever seen, and they had succeeded only in getting wet, miring their four-wheel drive in the mud, and not getting within a football field of a catchable trout.

For all I know, they may have been great anglers—better than us. But we had paid the money for local guides who knew that the *boca* of the Chimehuin would be fishable—in fact, perfect—when other streams were shut down.

Another thing with guides: There is nothing to be gained by trying to impress your guide with where you have fished and with whom. Having been on a stream with a famous fisherman does not make you a better angler any more than being in a concert hall with Dawn Upshaw makes you a world-class soprano. And it certainly does not impress the fish one way or the other.

This allied affliction is what I call Other Place Disease: You are fishing one place, and you keep observing how it reminds you of some other famous fishing spot. People can keep this talk up all afternoon. Again, it does nothing for your fishing, nor will it impress the guide. He or she has had many anglers who have fished many famous places, and they have talked ad infinitum. Furthermore, all this talk of your fishing travels takes your mind off the thing on which it should be concentrating: today's fishing.

Finally—and this is a corollary to the one about guys being unwilling to ask for directions—some of us find it equally hard to take constructive advice. If your guide offers advice, and usually this will start out very tentatively, try not to make an excuse about your fishing or, worse, be defensive. Be open to advice.

It is an axiom of psychoanalysis that "transfer-

ence"—the basis of the one-on-one relationship—
occurs in the first ten minutes of the first meeting
between doctor and patient. This may, in fact, be
true of all relationships. A good fishing guide will
begin to size up the angler right away. Is he talka-
tive? Can he take advice? Does he have much experience? You will get your money's worth if you
spend some time reading your guide as well. Remember that one of your jobs is to catch fish. The
other is to get the most out of your guide. He
knows something you don't, something that will
make you a better angler. And his job is to help you
get fish.

It's a win-win situation—if you make the most
of it. Seeking help and accepting it sometimes re-
quire overcoming a lot of macho acculturation, but
both are invaluable in the end.

Timing

**THERE MAY NEVER BE
A BETTER TIME THAN NOW**

In fishing, as in comedy, timing is everything. Put the best angler in the world on a stream where fish are not disposed to eat and you will see why Nature still holds the upper hand in the contest between man and his environment. Truly, as is written in Ecclesiastes, "To every thing there is a season." If you can, you should seek out your fishing when the season is ripe.

I understand that this cannot always be done. Real-life obligations such as jobs, kids' softball schedules, and parents' birthdays have a way of filling in the schedule, until the truth of the matter is that most of us fish whenever we can, which is not always when the fish want to play along.

Still, there is no question that if it is possible, you should try and pick your times. There is a right time to ask for a raise, to propose marriage, to go cross-country skiing, and there is a right time to fish.

But even then, if the water temperature isn't comfortable for the fish, you could be in the most famous fishing hole on Earth at the absolute right time of year and it is not worth getting out of your car. And you certainly don't want to get all geared up and lathered up with sunscreen for nothing. Much better to carry a little thermometer and stick it in the water. If the temperature is in the zone, fish. If it isn't, wait.

Thinking of time in a larger sweep, such as seasons, helps you predict if fish are likely—likely, not certain—to be in the neighborhood. I can tell you from experience that Florida in January is the hardest place and time to catch a bonefish. But Andros Island in March will forgive the first-timer. The Salmon Fly hatch on the Madison in early July or

the Green Drake hatch in June on the Delaware are
both guarantees of seeing big trout feeding on the
surface. Catching them, however, is still a matter of
good technique and the right fly. October in Montauk is when the peak of the striper migration passes
within casting distance of the beach, and in November, huge false albacore are found on the Outer
Banks of the Carolinas. Best of all, or most thrilling,
May and June in the Keys marks the passage of millions of tarpon along the shallow coral flats between
Biscayne Bay and Key West.

The precarious truth of right place, right time
was driven home late one spring when Islamorada
guide Allan Finkelman had a cancellation at the
peak of the tarpon run and invited me down to fish
it with him. The day before my plane left he had a
guy on board who could cast thirty feet if he had
the wind behind him but who somehow had man-
aged to hook six tarpon. I went to sleep assured that
I was, as the saying goes, in Fat City.

Next morning I caught the first plane out of
New York and drove hell-for-leather to Islamorada.

"You're not going to believe this," Allan said, "but late last night I got a call from a friend in Tavernier [a few miles north of Islamorada]. He said he had never seen so many tarpon—miles of them, maybe two hundred thousand, go past his house all afternoon."

"Hot damn!" I responded.

Then Allan brought down the hammer. "You don't understand. They were all leaving the Keys going north." Just like that, the migration had ended.

The day before, I would have been a tarpon millionaire; now I was just a fly fishing bum. Right place—at least it could've been right—but wrong time.

So along with the lesson that there is a right time to do things goes the additional fact of life that there are no guarantees. In fact, even in prime time you need the wind to be right, the tides to be right, the water temperature to be right, the rain to hold off, and on and on. Natural events—that is, hungry fish in the right place—depend on so many things.

If you get three days, even two days out of seven peak days that yield great fishing, count yourself fortunate. Some people go a whole year without one great day.

When things are great, anglers are known to enter a kind of fishing rapture. But once in this state, the minute things slow down they want to race off to the next spot. This is the piscatorial presumption that the fishing is always better on the other side of the lake. It isn't—and more times than not if you leave fish to find fish you will find nothing. When the going is good, stay with it.

One more thing about time is that you will never have more than you do right now. There are always more reasons not to go fishing than there are *to* fish. After all, everyone is too busy making a living and living a life. Seen in that light, you might never get to paint a picture, go to a concert, or take a fishing trip.

Sometimes you must just do it. For instance, I dreamed about spending a few weeks straight in Montauk and put the dream off every year. When I finally decided to do it I was as busy with life as ever, but I did it anyway. Best thing I ever did. Spending day after day with a fly rod in your hand will do wonders for your casting and your soul. You have none of that "I just got here and have to leave tomorrow" kind of anomie.

Life is not getting any longer, so whatever that dream is, treat yourself at least once. It will fill up your memory banks with sweet pictures for years to come. You might even learn that all the stuff that kept you from taking the time will still be there when you get back. . . . So why not do it again?

THE ESSENTIAL TRAITS
OF A FLY FISHER

We are all individuals, and there is as much variety in fly fishers as in any other group of people. Still, there are traits that we all share, and it is that constellation of likes, dislikes, and skills that makes us take up the fly rod and go to wild places.

LOVE OF NATURE

There is an old bluegrass gospel tune that comes to mind:

> If you look in the Bible
>
> In the book of Matthew
>
> In the 18th chapter and the 31st verse
>
> You can't get to heaven if you don't love your neighbor
>
> Because if you don't love your neighbor then you don't
>
> love God.

Likewise, you will never be a fly fisher if you don't love nature. No matter how good the fishing, you will spend more time looking at flowing water, mountain sunsets, diving birds, and clouds of mayflies than you will spend catching fish. In fact, I think the reason that I love fly fishing so much is that it is the thing that connects me to the energy, beauty, drama, and peace of Nature.

LOVING THE CAST

It is pretty evident from the first time you see a person fly fishing: The thing that makes it distinctive is the cast. It's like watching one of those multiple exposures of a golf swing or a tennis stroke, only with a fly rod you don't need a multiple exposure: The line itself is the visible and physical expression of an energy wave. When you execute it properly, it is as if your arm and fingers reach out a hundred feet with the grace of a ballerina gesturing with her arms. Casting is easy to learn, hard to master, and there are always ways to get better. Beauty, energy, and the constant challenge are a powerful attraction.

A BELIEF IN POSSIBILITY

I never go fishing without the belief that this could be the Big Day. Of course, driving rain, cold wind, and fishless hours can temper that enthusiasm, but I start every fishing session with the certainty that I am going to do well. That makes me, and all fly fishers, what they used to call "cockeyed optimists." Guilty as charged, but much better than being Captain Bringdown Pessimist.

READING WATER

To some, an expanse of water is a blank, unreadable slate. Pretty but unrevealing. A fly fisher can see currents and imagine what bait is doing in them and where gamefish lurk alongside them. Changes in water color signaling changes in depth, rip currents, rocks, eddies . . . in fact, every place where the speed or depth of water changes is what hunters call the Edge. Predators love the Edge, the place where one natural zone transitions to another and all gamefish are predators. So are we, which is why we have an instinctive affinity for Edges.

READING BIRDS

Birds like insects and bait as much as gamefish do. If you pay attention to birds and their behavior, it is like having a thousand Brittany spaniels on point in a grouse cover. When mayflies hatch at the end of the riffle, maybe a quarter-mile away, it's too far to see the rise of a trout but not too far to catch sunlight off the wings of a flock of sparrows as they dip and dive through the cloud of tasty insects. You know that trout are doing the same thing. On the ocean, a mass of gulls, gannets, or terns diving on the water means penned up baitfish underneath. And what pens up baitfish? Marauding gamefish. On a tarpon flat, even under a cloudy sky and with no visibility in the water, a flock of low-flying pelicans passing over the surface will always spook a pod of tarpon. They will "blow up," as the saying goes, with the commotion of a fair-sized depth charge. Even a lone highflying man-of-war bird over the Gulf Stream is probably in the exact place you find him because a marlin or sailfish is chasing bait below.

DREAMING ABOUT FLY FISHING

A dream, Dr. Freud tells us, is a wish fulfilled, a powerful wish. I often find myself dreaming of trout streams, of bonefish flats. Many times I dream I am back in my youth taking a walk from our house in a development in New Jersey and within minutes find myself in a secluded valley with a great looking trout stream running through it. Believe me, there was no trout stream in my neighborhood, but my psyche desperately wants to put one there. When I go on a fishing trip, I dream of the next day's fishing (it's always good). When I am housebound and stir crazy I have the same kind of dreams, often in the same setting. Perhaps Freud would find some deep psychosexual subtext in all of this . . . unless, of course, he fly fished. In which case he would have recognized that sometimes a fish can simply represent a fish.

PATIENCE

Even the greatest anglers spend more hours not catching fish than they spend catching fish. The best fishing of the day can be over in five minutes, but you wouldn't trade those five minutes for anything. So you must have patience—patience to drive long distances in a car or boat (sometimes both), patience to wait for a hatch, patience to wait out the tide, patience for a pod of fish to make it from a half-mile out right up to the shore. Fishing, as so much else in life, is a waiting game.

THE URGE FOR SOLITUDE

fly fishing isn't a team sport. From this a couple of things follow: First, no one is keeping score. Second, you can do it

all by yourself. Yes it is fun to have a fishing buddy along—
sometimes it is foolhardy not to—but you can also go down
to a stream by yourself, down to the shore by yourself, out in
a canoe by yourself. You are not isolated then. You have the
whole world for company: You simply don't have to put up
with the pecking orders, the backbiting, the endless blather,
the rejections, the hurly-burly of society. Instead, you can
draw on the reservoirs of peace and beauty that fill the
natural world and, if you are lucky, some of the juice that
comes from fighting a good fish.

CONCENTRATION

Fish do not want to be caught. They will do anything they can
to avoid it. The fly fisher must be alert, hypertuned at all
times, if there is to be any chance of success. Turn your head
for a moment and a fish can be on and off your fly. When you
are in that zone of concentration, every part of your being is a
nerve ending. Concentration on one thing in some strange
way can, if it is total enough, bring oneness with everything.
Sounds mystical, but I know it's true.

WHISTLING

"Whistle while you work . . ." goes the old song. I also think whistling while you fish is a good idea. I always have a song going through my head in every fishing session. Sometimes it is a song I like. Sometimes it is the Folger's coffee commercial. I have no control over it. But I do know that when I find myself endlessly whistling a tune, often unconsciously, then I am happy. So since I am always whistling while fishing, I can only conclude that fishing makes me happy. I guess this is probably true of anything that makes you happy that way . . . whistling is the litmus test.

NOT CARING ABOUT SIZE

Don't get me wrong: Big fish are great to catch, but they are not everything. I would much rather catch many smaller (smaller, but not pissant) fish on a fly than one humdinger on bait—quality of the experience and all that. You can fish the Everglades all day and your biggest bass on a fly may, on a good day, top three pounds. Not much compared to the hundred-pound tarpon fifty miles to the south. But the tarpon don't come with a hundred miles of sawgrass all around, scores of alligators lolling on the banks, every bird in creation. As in real estate, location plays a big role in fly fishing, and every natural place has its rewards. For example, I once fished the south fork of the Kern River in California. It is the home, the only home, of the golden trout. If you catch one anywhere else, it may be bigger, but it is an immigrant. On Golden Trout Creek, which feeds the Kern, a big fish is ten inches—but you know you have done the thing completely and right. So size matters, I suppose, but not more than other things. You make the connections to the rest of life.

l e s s o n   e l e v e n

Enough or Too Much?

**SIMPLICITY CAN BE THE KEY
TO SATISFACTION AND SUCCESS**

You can buy a lot of gear for fly fishing. You can have one rod for bluegill, one for bass, one for big trout, one for smallmouth, one for bonefish, one for tarpon. You can have travel versions that fit in a suitcase or two-piecers that go in baggage on planes. There are lightweight, midweight, and heavyweight waders; ditto for raingear. At least count, you have your choice of forty thousand fly patterns, and there are waterproof, big and little, magnetic, and wooden boxes to carry them in your long, short, mesh, or solid vest.

In the beginning you are going to want everything. But as the years go by I have come more to embrace the motto of the ancient Athenians, "Everything in proportion and nothing in excess," or, put more colloquially, Less is more.

Art Flick, the author of the shortest and certainly clearest book on fly selection, tried to get the number of flies you need to fish the Catskill streams down to about ten. This book had a great influence on me. Nowadays when I go fishing, I try to take as few rods, as few flies, and as little gear as possible. I will carry this to extremes that work for me but which horrify some of my angling friends.

For instance, last fall the herring made their run down the East Coast. The biggest bass of the year—in fact, of my life—followed in their wake. I fished well into a warm December, and one afternoon I caught a forty-five-inch, thirty-five-pound bass on the fly—an all-time record for me. I was fishing one of the Orvis T-3 rods, an eight-weight. As I often do with fly rods, I overlined it; that is, I used a heavier line than the manufacturer called for. With a ten-weight sink tip I was able to handle the

wind and get the fly down to the level of the bass.
When the striper took, he gave me a long and satisfying fight on light tackle. I could have had two
rods on the boat, an eight-weight and a ten; instead
I took one rod and two reels. Less gear, less to
forget, less to break, less to have to deal with.

Similar situation with flies. Although I have
made much of proper imitation, it remains true that
a well-presented fly is, in my experience, usually
much more important than the exact right fly. True,
on a spring creek with multiple hatches, fish can be
impossibly finicky, but on most free stone streams
or in saltwater you will be surprised by how many
fish respond to the same fly. I have caught bass on
tarpon flies, bonefish on smallmouth flies. The trick
here is that wherever you go, whatever you do, have
a few flies you believe in, flies that have worked for
you. They may not be the rightest of the right for
the situation, but if you have confidence in them,
somehow the fish know it and will cooperate.

With waders and clothing, I travel with layers
rather than with different outfits. Running to make

airport connections, your arms and back will thank you for the lighter load. The general rule is, Take the minimum and then simplify even more. In philosophy this is called Ockham's razor, named after a medieval mathematician and cleric who laid down the proposition that if there is more than one solution to a problem, the simplest one is the correct one.

To that medieval monk I offer a thankful "Amen," in fishing and in everything.

THE SOUNDS
OF FLY FISHING

I can hear the sound of a trout feeding the same way a mother hears the cough of her child three rooms away. You become attuned to things and tune the rest of the world out. Fly fishing is a visual sport, a tactile sport, but it also involves all the senses. When you are aware of the sounds of fly fishing, nothing else intrudes—at least for that blissful moment.

RUNNING WATER

Burbling brook, running stream, crashing surf, rushing tide—there is music in water. Each one an overture, a promise (or at least the possibility) of fish on the rise, on the feed, ready to take. The primal moment for me is walking through the woods and first hearing the low susurrus, the faint whisper of running water in the distance, still so far off that it could be a stream or it could be the wind. Then—yes!—there is no mistaking the gentle babbling of water flowing over stones, soft as a lullaby, exciting as fireworks.

THE RISE

Just before sunset, it is quiet on the stream. As the summer air cools, bringing the water temperature down with it, mayflies start their flight. And then, as surely as trout follow food, you can hear a fish, a big one, sloppily slurping a struggling mayfly. One second it is a fluttering jewel on the water, and the next it disappears to the hollow sound of water and air being sucked in by a rising fish. Then another fish rises farther out in the stream. Then another. They sip, they slurp, they set up a rhythm, and I know that all I need is the right fly and the right cast because these fish are calling to me.

LAWNMOWERS

When I was young I caddied—briefly—at a local golf course. The greens were cut by a lawnsman with a hand-pushed mower. It made a whirring, chewing kind of sound as it clipped the tops of the lush grass. Then came power mowers, power blowers, electric-powered golf carts, and powered everything else. The handmower was a sound that

I forgot about for many years until I began to fish false albacore. On the right tide, these swift predators will line up along a rip and pin bait against it. Then, like a platoon of lawnmowers, they will line up along the whole width of the bait school and chew their way through it. At fifty feet it sounds just like the blades of the old mower at the Montclair Golf Club.

BARBARIC YAWPS

A sound arises when the fish are hitting—doesn't matter what kind, could be bluefish, striped bass, albacore, yellowfin, weakfish. When this happens, when a whole bunch of fish throw caution to the winds (actually, they throw it to the waves) and pounce on a bait school, sometimes there is a group of anglers ready and waiting. First one angler connects with a high "Yippee!" then a couple more let fly with joyful unprintables, then every boat and every angler on the shore is screaming, yahooing, giving conflicting shouted directives, whistling, cursing a blue streak. It all blends in to one happy shout, a group yell of pure pleasure.

"DADDY, WHAT DO I DO NOW?"

A child not catching fish is a bored child, one not very likely to share Daddy's passion. Ah, but then a fish hits. You hear a squeak and a laugh, followed by the realization that "Ohmygod, this thing is for real and it wants to fight me!" At that point, your child is hooked on fishing and the plea for help and advice confirms this and swells a father's heart. I would be lying if I said I enjoy it more than catching a fish myself, but almost.

THE SCREE OF GULLS

Gulls squawking on the shore are not particularly mellifluous. In fact, they kind of get on my nerves. But mix in the sound of breakers and send those gulls fifty yards off shore, where they gather in a tight diving screaming ball over frothing baitfish, well . . . then you have the certainty that something drove those baitfish to the surface, something that you want to catch. The gulls signal the beginning of mayhem and carnage, and something in your blood rises as you race toward the sound.

TOM-TOMS

Once I was sitting in a skiff, having a day's-end beer with a few other anglers in similar boats. Before the sun set, the moon came up, and as it did it seemed to pull up an acre of bass—maybe ten acres. Thousands of them feeding on the surface. They made a *whoosh-whoosh* as they cruised through the bait. When we made our way into the heart of the frenzy, the fish paid us no heed. They kept coming head and tail through the school. Hundreds of them flapped their tails against the sides of our boats, which they regarded as nothing more than a nuisance. The bass sounded as if they were pounding war drums to urge us all to battle.

WHISTLING GUIDES

The prime objective of the cast is to deliver the fly to the fish. But there are casts and there are casts. Just as you can drive to Detroit in a used pick-up truck or a just-off-the-boat Mercedes, the way something gets to its destination is important. Many fly fishers—make that all fly fishers—will at one time or another waste a lot of motion and energy.

As it is with swinging a baseball bat or a tennis racquet, there is a sweet spot, best enlisted by a smooth, sweet stroke. You know when you have nailed it because the ball jumps off the bat or the racquet. Likewise with a fly rod, when you really smoke a cast you stop your power stroke high and the line whooshes out through the guides, quietly but steadily giving off a sound somewhere between a whistle and a click. It is the sound of a satisfied rod and a beautiful cast.

SINGING REELS

Any time a fly fishing author is stuck for a description of the exhilarating moment when a fish takes line on a long run, the go-to phrase is "a singing reel." The reel doesn't really sing. It usually clicks, but a fast-moving fish will make the reel move so fast that the pitch gets higher and higher. It's just one note, I suppose, so that doesn't qualify it as a song, but it is the music of success, the underscoring for the peak moment for any fly fisher: when a great fish is on and testing the mettle of angler and tackle.

SILENCE

Yes, there is a sound to silence. If you don't believe me, listen to the stillness before dawn on a Montana creek, the quiet when the wind dies on Florida Bay as the sun sinks. There is the total absence of sound on the lakes of central Finland in the middle of the short Arctic night, the quiet when a wind-driven squall has rushed across a stream followed by the steamy stillness of the return of humid summer heat. The world is full of sound over sound. To experience silence is to appreciate both sound and its absence. You feel part of the world—like the whole world or perhaps the only person in it.

The Art of Inquiry

DON'T LET ON HOW BADLY YOU WANT
TO KNOW, AND SOMEONE MAY TELL YOU

You're a stranger in a strange town reputed to have great fishing. You walk into the tackle shop and ask, "Where are they biting?" The guy takes out the map and makes a few Xs at the same spot he marks for everyone who asks. Not very helpful. You could have done just as well by looking at a roadmap.

There is an art to asking questions, an art to following up. As a journalist you learn this early, if you are going to have any success at all. As an angler, the same principles hold.

You must gather information in bits, from here

and from there, remembering that in fishing, as in combat, a frontal assault is often anticipated and easily repelled.

So, say you are a stranger and you want a clue from the locals. Start at the gas station. First rule: Pay in cash. If you use a credit card, there is no one to talk to, and you want human contact.

"Nice day for fishing," you say to the guy who takes your money. If he agrees, you are probably addressing a fellow angler.

"You know where I can buy some bait?" is a good follow-up. It shows you are willing to pump some more money into the local economy. And the follow-up follow-up is, "Any recommendation [for bait]?"

Leave it at that. Any more questioning and you will be perceived, rightly, as someone pumping for information.

Next stop, the bait store. "Are they still taking X [whatever it was that was recommended at the gas station]?" This shows you know something about what is happening in the area, and it also shows you are deferring to the advice of the expert at the bait shop. Now take out your wallet and buy some bait, also some hooks, or sinkers, or maybe a lure. I realize that you are a fly fisher and you will not need any of this, but the ten or fifteen dollars you spend will be well worth it if it leads you to fish.

Now comes the moment of truth: where to fish. "Say, I don't want to know anybody's secret spots, but could you recommend a place where I have a shot at a few fish?"

In all likelihood, this question will elicit a recommendation of one of the two or three places that every local knows. Heavily pressured, to be sure, but at least a place where fish have been caught within living memory.

And so the story goes. You go to the recommended spot. You ask the angler there how he is doing. Then maybe about the bait. Then maybe he tells you that Joe Smith caught one on something else down by Johnson's pasture. Then the lady at the grocery store tells you how to find Johnson's pasture, and then you find the fish.

It is a long way round, but, as in police investigation or reporting, if you want to find things out from strangers, get your information a little bit at a time. Take your time, don't appear too eager, and be as nonchalant as possible. Nobody likes a nosy stranger.

Home

**HOME IS MORE OF A FEELING,
RATHER THAN A PLACE**

Jim Clark must be about sixty-five years old. I think he has fished the East End of Long Island for no less the sixty years. He is big as a full-back, still paddles his kayak ten miles every day of the year (provided the wind is below twenty knots), and is the first guy with whom I fly fished Montauk and the Hamptons.

I have fished the world. Whenever I ask Jim if he is interested in a trip, he answers, "Why would I want to?"

Jim is one of those anglers who loves his home water, knows it like he knows the faces of his chil-

dren, and who appreciates everything about its seasons, its wildlife, its anglers, even its people.

There is something to be said for home waters.
Home itself is the most comforting word in our lan-
guage. You could opt for *mother* or *love*, but sometimes there are a few psychological issues with
family and lovers. Home is warmth, familiarity, memories. Soldiers want to go home. Prisoners dream of
home. Salmon return to their home streams, and Jim
fishes near home.

Apart from the practical point that when you
fish near home you don't have far to go, there is satisfaction in acquiring a deep knowledge of a place.
Nuance, the way light falls at three in the afternoon
in the different seasons, the sounds of birds leaving
in autumn and coming in spring, the meaning—
bred into your bones—of north winds, south winds,
early snow, daisies . . . all of these build, over the
course of a lifetime, into a second skin of experience, memories, and knowledge.

And then, of course, the fishing. You know,
without even knowing that you know because it is

instinct, how the water colors when the depth is right for fish, how a storm moves the bars or blows out the lips of trout pools or piles up the lily pads on one side of a lake. And when you see this, you know where the fish should be. Rising barometers tell your internal barometer what to expect, or at least what it is reasonable to hope for.

Home is where you feel safe when your children go fishing. Home is where you know when it is unsafe. Home is where every one of your friends has a fish tale about a place you know. Home is where no one cuts you slack about your own embroidered fishing yarns.

You can have more than one home. When I go to New Orleans or Buenos Aires or Rome, I feel I am at home, a place that was one of "my places." So too, with fishing, I feel at home at Montauk, at home in the Everglades, at home on the Chimehuin in Argentina, on the Ashokan Reservoir in the Catskills, on Slough Creek in Yellowstone Park. I do not know those waters the way Jim Clark knows Montauk, but I feel comfortable and at ease on them and near them.

There are anglers who travel the world constantly, never finding a home port until they are as parched for home as the Ancient Mariner becalmed on a cloudless sea. Home is anywhere, then, where the quality of the experience, if only for a moment, makes you feel "I have always been here."

In a way, you have always been there. Fishing is a contest between humans and nature, a drama that has been playing out for hundreds of thousands of years. Fly fishing, to my way of thinking, is the most beautiful way to play a role in that drama—sometimes tragedy, sometimes farce, but always riveting.

May you find something that does the same for you.